the
RAMADAN
Family
COOKBOOK

the RAMADAN *Family* COOKBOOK

80 recipes for enjoying with loved ones

ANISA KAROLIA

Contents

✦ ・・・・✦・・・・ ✦

Introduction

Welcome to *The Ramadan Family Cookbook*, a collection of family-friendly recipes that will help nourish you and your loved ones during the blessed month and throughout the remainder of the year. This book is your culinary companion, which will help you create not just meals but also memorable moments around the table, and forge connections and bonds from spending quality time together in the kitchen and through the shared passion of cooking.

For me and my family, and for Muslims around the world, Ramadan is a special time that holds a beautiful place in our hearts, a month we long for as we come together to observe fasting, offer prayers and engage in acts of charity, kindness, self-improvement, self-discipline and self-reflection. Ramadan is also about practising patience and self-control and is seen as a time for cleansing the heart and soul of negative qualities and seeking forgiveness.

Ramadan holds a lot of special memories for me. I knew Ramadan was around the corner when my mum and aunty started preparing savouries together for the blessed month, and when the grocery shops and supermarkets were packed with people rushing to buy ingredients – samosa and spring roll wraps, puff pastry sheets – before everything sold out.

There is always an incredible buzz and vibe around this time. Ramadan encourages unity and togetherness. People take care to create a welcoming atmosphere in their homes; hospitality, warmth and mindfulness are extended during this holy month, and we embrace the values of compassion and kindness.

When I was younger, I remember my parents would wake me and my brother Suhayl for suhoor, a pre-dawn breakfast. We would sit for a few minutes with a blurry-eyed look on our faces until some tea and eggs or toast were placed in front of us. Even as children, we still wanted to maximise the experience and fullness of Ramadan just as much as everyone else, especially as it only came around once a year. Although it was early in the morning, we understood why suhoor was important for all Muslims who observe the fasts in the month of Ramadan. At school with friends, we would chat about what time we woke up and what we ate; suhoor and iftar were always the talking point in the school playground with others who observed Ramadan.

This special month is also about sharing food with your friends and family. I was fortunate to have my aunties, uncles and grandparents nearby, and my dear mum would send me over with plates of food that I helped prepare – samosas, pakoras, desserts – and they would send food over too. Traditions like these are very common still today, and you can often smell the delicious food wafting through the streets either from kitchen windows or from freshly prepared plates in the hands of those delivering to neighbours.

As the sun set and the call to prayer echoed through the air (Maghrib), my father and brother would make their way to the local mosque for congregational prayers. Once we had all finished our evening prayers, families and communities would gather to break their fast (iftar), offering thanks to the Almighty and starting with the traditional dates and water.

We would then gather around the dinner table for the main meal. A typical iftar spread would consist of a combination of different food groups and flavours – one or two varieties of starters, for example, such as samosas and pakoras, a main dish such as chicken curry and chapati, a light, creamy fruity custard for dessert, and a refreshing drink like a strawberry or rose milkshake. The menu would change every other day.

To this day, the same tradition is carried forward. Suhoor is still a lively time in my home – our three children wake up to take part in the pre-dawn breakfast. My husband Adam usually gets downstairs first, flicks the kettle on and helps make a start on preparing the breakfast, and the children also like to get involved in the meal prep.

Our iftar meal is also unchanged. The kitchen comes alive, and is noisy with the sound of dishes and utensils, busy and vibrant with the colours and aroma of cooking and preparing food. The whole experience creates a feeling of comfort and togetherness with my family. It brings back a lot of happy memories of my Ramadan as a child, a beautiful reminder to cherish the moments whether during occasions like Ramadan or in everyday life.

Having family around is beautiful. It provides a foundation of love and support and this binds generations together. Having my dear mother and father-in-law join us for iftar creates an opportunity for them to share their stories and experiences. It's a sign of unity and respect and adds value to the joy and bonding you experience during this special time; the love that comes from these gatherings is deeply fulfilling.

I think it's important that everyone contributes to preparing the food. Not only does this lighten the workload and allow more time for relaxation and prayer for everyone, but it also promotes teamwork and shared responsibility for the well-being of the entire family and shows care and consideration for one another.

I also like to involve my children in the meal preparation and pass down traditional recipes, cooking techniques and practices that I have picked up from my parents and grandparents. In turn, the children feel a sense of accomplishment and satisfaction that they have taken part in this ritual, making the iftar and suhoor experience even more rewarding and at the same time learning some life skills.

I am forever grateful to the Almighty for blessing us with so much variety of food and for being able to see the happy faces of my family around the dinner table, eating, chatting and exchanging stories. We can so easily take these things for granted, but these moments remind me to appreciate everything, and make me think about the less fortunate, who are not so lucky to have food and family around them.

I hope you feel the passion and excitement that I've put into all these delightful recipes for you with each written word. May they not only fill your plates, but also your heart and soul. Enjoy your journey of cooking!

Anisa x

The Perfect Menu Ideas

Family Feast

Starter
Creamy Chicken Moons   20

Main
Lamb Nihari (pictured)   84

Dessert
Zarda, Sweet Rice   107

Drink
Roseberry Mocktail   158

Eid Meal

Starter
Peri-Peri Chicken   34
Puff Pastries (pictured)

Main
Lamb Akhni   71

Dessert
No-Bake Rasmalai   144
Milk Cake

Drink
Mango Lassi   166

When you're cooking for a crowd it can be hard to know what goes well together. Here, I've suggested some of my favourite dish combinations.

Veggie Iftar Meal

Starter

Spicy Vegetable Samosas   36

Main

Cauliflower, Potato & Pea Curry (pictured)   104

Dessert

Avocado Surprise   154

Drink

Strawberry Milkshake   165

Healthier Iftar Meal

Starter

Lamb Kebabs with Mint Dip (pictured)   61

Main

Grilled Chipotle Chicken Skewers with Mexican-Inspired Savoury Rice   49, 80

Dessert

Summer Berry Pavlova   132
Fruity Custard   146

Drink

Mango & Passion Fruit Mocktail   160

CROWD-PLEASING
Bites

✦ • • • • • ✦ • • • • • ✦

Savoury snacks have always been a part
of my Indian heritage. This chapter includes
generations-old recipes alongside some modern
twists. Whether enjoyed with a cup of chai
or shared during festive gatherings, these
tantalising bites carry stories of love and
connection, laughter and cherished moments.

 The Creamy Chicken Moons, Lamb Samosas, Veggie
Paneer Spring Rolls and Peri-Peri Chicken Puff Pastries
can all be made in large batches and kept in the
freezer. Arrange them uncooked on a baking sheet
then freeze until hard. Store in plastic freezer bags
in small quantities, then defrost and bake or fry
when required.

Kheema Stuffed Parathas

MAKES
6-7

Prep 30 minutes
Cook 5 minutes

Also known as Mughlai paratha in the Indian subcontinent, or murtabak in the Middle East, this dish is made with aromatic spiced lamb mince with onions and fresh herbs stuffed in a homemade flatbread and deep-fried until golden and flaky. My grandmother made these when she had samosa filling left over and didn't want to waste it. Serve with fresh lemon wedges and a sauce or dip of your choice.

Ingredients

250g chapati flour
50g plain flour, plus extra for rolling
1 tablespoon margarine
180–200ml hot water
oil for deep-frying, plus extra for kneading
2 eggs, beaten, for egg wash
salt, to taste

FILLING
1 x quantity filling from Lamb
Samosas (see page 31)

Method

Place the flours in a large bowl with a little salt, add the margarine and rub it into the flour with your fingertips for about 3 minutes until the mixture resembles breadcrumbs. Make a well in the middle of the flour and slowly pour in the hot water, a little at a time, just enough to form a soft dough. Knead the dough for about a minute until there is no flour left at the bottom of the bowl. The dough shouldn't be too sticky or too dry.

Transfer the dough to a lightly floured surface and knead with your hands for about 5 minutes until it becomes soft and pliable. You can put a little oil on your hands while kneading so it doesn't stick to your fingers.

Divide the dough into 6–7 equal-sized balls. Pop them back into the bowl and cover with a cloth to prevent them drying out.

Using a rolling pin, roll out the balls on a lightly floured surface into circles about 15cm in diameter and 1mm thick. Brush the egg wash over each circle, including the edges.

Place 3 tablespoons of the mince filling in the centre of each circle. Fold two sides into the middle to meet and fold the other two so they just touch to seal. See page 33 for how to do this.

Heat the oil for deep-frying in a large saucepan until it reaches 180°C.

Fry the parathas for 2 minutes on each side until you notice small bubbles appearing on the surface and they turn golden in colour. You will need to do this in small batches, making sure not to overcrowd the pan. Drain on kitchen paper.

Creamy Chicken Moons

MAKES
30

Prep 40 minutes
Cook 30 minutes

These delectable crescent-shaped wonders are soft and saucy on the inside, and crunchy on the outside, they're a true delight that will win the hearts of everyone who tastes them.

Ingredients

2 tablespoons oil

1 onion, finely diced

500g chicken breasts, cut into small pieces

1 teaspoon ginger paste

1 teaspoon garlic paste

1 teaspoon green chilli paste

1 teaspoon ground cumin

6 tablespoons sweetcorn kernels

one small red pepper, cut into 1cm cubes

one small green pepper, cut into 1cm cubes

5g fresh coriander, finely chopped

3–4 eggs, beaten

250g shop-bought golden breadcrumbs

oil, for deep-frying

salt, to taste

WHITE SAUCE

50g unsalted butter

50g plain flour

½ teaspoon black pepper

½ teaspoon grated nutmeg (optional)

600ml milk

DOUGH

250g plain flour, plus 2 tbsp for flour paste and extra for rolling

30g butter

250ml hot water

Method

Heat the oil in a large wok over a low-medium heat. Add the onions and fry for 5 minutes until soft and translucent. Add the chicken, ginger and garlic paste, green chilli paste, ground cumin and salt, and give everything a mix. Cover and cook over a medium heat for 20 minutes until no moisture remains. Stir in the sweetcorn and red and green peppers, cook for 5–6 minutes until the peppers have softened slightly, then remove from the heat and set aside to cool completely.

To make the white sauce, melt the butter in a large saucepan, then add the flour, black pepper, nutmeg, if using, and salt to taste. Stir continuously until a paste forms. Pour in the milk a little at a time, stirring constantly. Bring to a simmer and continue cooking over a low heat for about 5 minutes until the sauce is smooth and thickened.

Pour the sauce over the chicken mixture and mix well. You can add more or less depending on how saucy you want the mixture. Stir through the chopped coriander.

To make the dough, place the flour in a large bowl with a little salt. Add the butter and rub it into the flour with your fingertips. Pour the hot water in slowly until the mix comes together into a soft dough. Divide the dough into 2 pieces.

Roll out 1 piece of the dough on a floured surface to around 3mm thickness. Using a

large cutter, cut out round circles. Take 1 heaped tablespoon of the chicken mixture and place it in the centre of each circle. Combine 2 tablespoons of plain flour with 4 tablespoons of water to create a flour paste, then use this to brush the edges of the circles and seal well. Repeat the process with the second piece of dough.

Place the beaten egg in a shallow bowl and the breadcrumbs in a separate shallow bowl. Dip the moons into

beaten egg, and then coat in breadcrumbs, making sure the moons are completely covered.

Heat the oil for deep-frying in a large saucepan until it reaches 180°C. Drop a breadcrumb into the oil – if it sizzles, the oil is ready. Fry the moons in batches for 2–3 minutes on each side until golden all over, then drain on kitchen paper. They are best eaten fresh on the day they are fried.

Fish Cutlets

Prep 30 minutes
Cook 8 minutes

MAKES
20

These flavourful and crispy fried savouries are perfect as a starter or appetiser. The fish is steamed, delicately flaked and lightly spiced, and the potatoes bind the mixture together and enhance the texture. Coating the patties in breadcrumbs before frying adds a satisfyingly crunchy bite! Serve with lemon wedges and dip in your favourite sauce.

Ingredients

2 large potatoes, peeled and cut into 2.5cm chunks
2 cod fillets
5 garlic cloves, finely chopped
5 fresh green chillies, finely chopped
1 teaspoon ground cumin
1 teaspoon ground coriander
1 teaspoon hot paprika
1 teaspoon dried dill
1 teaspoon ground black pepper
1 lemon, ½ juiced and ½ cut into wedges, to garnish
5g fresh coriander, finely chopped
3 spring onions, finely chopped
4 eggs, beaten
200g golden breadcrumbs
500ml sunflower oil, for frying
salt, to taste

Method

Bring a saucepan of water to the boil, add the potatoes and cook for 20 minutes, or until tender. Drain well.

Meanwhile, put at least 7cm of water in the bottom of a steamer, cover and bring to the boil. Lay the fish on the steamer's rack, making sure the rack is not touching the water, and cover again. Steam for 8–10 minutes, or until the fish is cooked through. Flake the fish with a fork.

In a large bowl, mash the cooked potatoes with a potato masher, leaving some lumps to add texture. Add the flaked fish, chopped garlic and chillies, ground cumin and coriander, hot paprika, dried dill, black pepper, juice of ½ lemon, fresh coriander and spring onions. Mix everything together – you can use a spoon, but I prefer to use my hands, as I find it's quicker and combines all the ingredients properly.

Divide the mixture into 20 equal-sized balls and press down lightly to form circular patties.

Place the eggs and breadcrumbs in separate bowls. Dip each cutlet into the beaten eggs, then into the breadcrumbs. If desired, you can repeat the process and double coat them; this prevents the mixture from bursting while frying.

Pour the oil into a large frying pan over a medium heat and heat until it reaches 180°C. Fry the cutlets in batches for 4 minutes on each side until golden. Drain on kitchen paper.

NOTE

This dish works best if you fry just before serving.

You can add more or fewer fresh chillies, depending on your taste.

Hot & Saucy BBQ Wings

MAKES

15

Prep 10 minutes
Marinate 1 hour
Cook 10 minutes

Tender, juicy chicken wings, dripping with a tantalising hot barbecue sauce. My children love these wings and are they are often on the menu with a side of wedges. Trust me, every bite will have you reaching for more.

Ingredients

15 chicken wings
200ml buttermilk
50ml pickle juice
1 teaspoon ground black pepper
oil, for deep-frying
1 tablespoon chives

BBQ SAUCE
60g butter
100g brown sugar
200g tomato ketchup
3 tablespoons hot chilli sauce
1 tablespoon mustard
1 tablespoon apple cider vinegar
1 tablespoon Worcestershire sauce
1 teaspoon smoked paprika
120ml water

FLOUR MIX
240g plain flour
2 tablespoons cornflour
1 teaspoon smoked paprika
1 teaspoon chilli powder
1 teaspoon garlic granules
1 teaspoon onion granules
1 teaspoon ground black pepper
salt, to taste

Method

Place the chicken wings in a large bowl and pour over the buttermilk, pickle juice and black pepper. Set aside in the fridge for 1 hour.

For the BBQ sauce, melt the butter in a medium saucepan, then add the brown sugar, tomato ketchup, hot chilli sauce, mustard, apple cider vinegar, Worcestershire sauce, paprika and water. Simmer gently over a low heat until the sauce starts to bubble, then keep stirring for 2–3 minutes. The sauce will thicken slightly.

Make the flour mix in a large dish. Add plain flour, cornflour, smoked paprika, chilli powder, garlic granules, onion granules, black pepper and salt, and mix together.

One at a time, coat the wings in the flour mix and shake off any excess. You can double coat if you like for a crispier texture.

Heat the oil for deep-frying in a large saucepan until it reaches 180°C. Fry the wings for about 5 minutes until golden and crisp, then drain on kitchen paper.

Pour over the BBQ sauce, making sure the wings are completely covered and sprinkle over the chives.

Classic Smashburgers

Prep 20 minutes
Cook 5 minutes

MAKES
6

Mouth-watering, succulent smashburgers are lightly seasoned, yet every bite is packed with flavour. These are my two sons' favourite, and they insisted on adding this recipe to the book. They are super simple to prepare and perfect for your whole family, especially the burger lovers, as this recipe gives the perfect balance of crispy edges and juicy tenderness. Of course, these are best accompanied by chips.

Ingredients

600g beef mince (20% fat)
1 teaspoon black pepper
1 teaspoon garlic granules
1 teaspoon onion granules
oil
6 brioche buns
lettuce leaves
1 salad tomato, sliced
1 red onion, sliced into rings
6 cheese slices, your favourite type
salt, to taste

BURGER SAUCE
4 tablespoons tomato ketchup
4 tablespoons mayonnaise
2 tablespoons chilli sauce
1 tablespoon Dijon mustard
1 pickled gherkin, finely diced

NOTE
You could also make mini patties and use mini brioche buns. These are perfect for parties and get-togethers.

Method

To make the burger sauce, combine all the ingredients in a bowl and set aside.

Season the mince with the black pepper, garlic granules, onion granules and salt and mix everything together. Divide the mixture into 6 equal-sized balls, weighing approximately 115g each.

Brush a large cast-iron skillet or stainless-steel pan with a little oil and heat on a medium heat for 2–3 minutes. You want the pan to be hot. Place 2 balls on the pan and, using a large metal spatula, press down firmly on each one until they are roughly 13cm in diameter and 1cm thick.

Cook without moving the patties until a deep brown crust develops around the edges. This will take about 2 minutes as they're quite thin patties. With the edge of the spatula, flip the patties over and cook for another 2 minutes, until browned. Place the cheese on top at this point and remove from the heat.

Place a dollop of burger sauce onto the bun bases, add lettuce leaves, tomato slices and onion rings, then transfer the patties on top, cheese side up, and add more burger sauce to finish, if desired. Place the bun lids on top.

Onion Bhajiyas

Prep 20 minutes
Cook 6 minutes

MAKES
15

The humble onion bhajiya is probably the most popular Indian savoury snack. Sharp and pungent slices of onions in a spiced chickpea batter and deep-fried to crispy, golden-brown perfection, bhajiyas are a memorable treat. In my home, we often eat them with freshly made custard, especially during Ramadan, and love to share them with friends and family.

Ingredients

2 onions, finely sliced

125g fresh fenugreek leaves, chopped, stems removed

5g fresh coriander, finely chopped

1 teaspoon ground cumin

1 teaspoon ground coriander

½ teaspoon turmeric powder

1 teaspoon garlic paste

1 teaspoon green chilli paste

½ teaspoon baking powder

1 heaped tablespoon rice flour

200g chickpea flour

about 200ml water

oil, for deep-frying

salt, to taste

Method

Place the onions in a large bowl with the fenugreek, fresh coriander, ground cumin, ground coriander, turmeric powder, garlic paste, green chilli paste, baking powder, rice flour, chickpea flour and salt. Pour in enough water to hold the mixture together – it shouldn't be too thick or too thin.

Heat the oil for deep-frying in a large saucepan until it reaches 180°C. Drop a breadcrumb into the oil – if it sizzles, the oil is ready.

Add tablespoonfuls of the mixture to the hot oil and fry in batches for 2–3 minutes on each side until golden all over, then drain on kitchen paper. They are best eaten fresh on the day they are fried.

Veggie Paneer Spring Rolls

MAKES
20

Prep 30 minutes
Cook 10 minutes

A mouth-watering medley of fresh colourful vegetables, soft creamy paneer and aromatic spices, all wrapped in a crispy, golden spring roll. The fusion of Indian paneer and Asian spring rolls brings together the best of both worlds. These spring rolls are truly irresistible and will be sure to tantalise your taste buds.

Ingredients

2 tablespoons oil, plus extra for deep-frying
1 large onion, finely sliced
100g white cabbage, shredded
1 carrot, julienned
1 teaspoon cumin seeds
1 teaspoon garlic paste
1 teaspoon green chilli paste
3 tablespoons diced red pepper
3 tablespoons diced green pepper
6 tablespoons tinned sweetcorn, drained
200g paneer, grated
5g fresh coriander, finely chopped
1 spring onion, finely sliced
1 teaspoon ground cumin
1 teaspoon Kashmiri chilli powder
1 teaspoon chilli powder
3 tablespoons chilli sauce
1 teaspoon chilli flakes
1 tablespoon sesame seeds
1 teaspoon black pepper
2 tablespoons plain flour
20 spring roll wrappers, about 15cm square
salt, to taste

Method

Heat the oil in a wok on a high heat and add the onions, cabbage, carrots, cumin seeds, garlic and chilli paste. Stir, cover the wok, and cook for 2–4 minutes until the cabbage has softened slightly.

Add the peppers, sweetcorn, paneer, coriander, spring onion, ground cumin, Kashmiri chilli powder, chilli powder, chilli sauce, chilli flakes, sesame seeds and black pepper and season with salt. Toss well to ensure everything is evenly coated, and stir-fry for 2 minutes. Leave the mixture to cool completely.

Make a flour paste by mixing the flour and 4 tablespoons of water in a small bowl to a smooth consistency.

Place one of the spring roll wrappers on a flat surface with a corner facing towards you. Arrange 2 tablespoons of the filling in a line across the wrapper about 5cm up from the corner that is closest to you. Roll the bottom corner over the filling, then fold in both sides of the wrapper. See page 33 for how to do this. Continue rolling away from you until you have a neat cigar shape. Use a pastry brush to brush a little of the flour paste under the corner of the wrapper to seal it.

Heat the oil for deep-frying in a large saucepan on a medium-high heat until it reaches 180°C. Fry the spring rolls in batches for 2–3 minutes on each side until golden all over, then drain on kitchen paper. They are best eaten fresh on the day they are fried.

Lamb Samosas

Prep 30 minutes
Cook 20 minutes

MAKES

25–30

One of my fondest childhood food memories was the ever-present plate of hot samosas and pot of karak chai whenever we visited relatives. I think this was a tradition in most Indian households, and, of course, it was no different in our home. Samosas are perfect for any gathering, and though traditionally deep-fried, these can also be air-fried or baked in the oven.

Ingredients

500g lamb mince
½ teaspoon cumin seeds
1 teaspoon ground black pepper
½ teaspoon salt
1 teaspoon green chilli paste
1 teaspoon ginger paste
1 teaspoon garlic paste
2 tablespoons oil, plus extra for deep-frying
1 teaspoon ground cumin
1 teaspoon ground coriander
1 teaspoon chilli powder
½ teaspoon garam masala
30g frozen petit pois
3 tablespoons finely chopped spring onion
1 onion, finely diced
5g fresh coriander, finely chopped
5g fresh mint, finely chopped
2 tablespoons plain flour
25–30 samosa leaves

Method

Heat the mince in a wok on a medium heat with the cumin seeds, black pepper, salt, chilli paste, ginger and garlic paste. Cook for about 15 minutes, stirring occasionally, then cover and continue cooking until no moisture is left, about 20 minutes. Add the oil, ground cumin, ground coriander, chilli powder, garam masala and petit pois. Stir, and cook for 2 minutes, then set aside to cool.

When cool, add the spring onion, onions, fresh coriander and mint and mix together.

Make a flour paste by mixing the flour and 4 tablespoons of water in a small bowl to a smooth consistency.

Lay a samosa leaf on a work surface with one short end facing you, and fold to form a triangular pocket. See page 32 for how to do this. Fill the pocket with 1 heaped teaspoon of filling, then use a pastry brush to brush some of the flour paste on the top of the filled triangle. Continue to wrap the samosa, brushing paste between the layers to make a neat triangular parcel. Repeat with the remaining samosa leaves and filling.

Heat the oil for deep-frying in a large saucepan on a medium-high heat until it reaches 180°C. Fry the samosas in batches for 2–3 minutes on each side until golden all over, then drain on kitchen paper. They are best eaten fresh on the day they are fried.

How to fold

Follow these diagrams to fold the perfect samosa and spring roll. As with most things, practice makes perfect so if you don't succeed first time, keep trying! It's lovely to teach these techniques to children too, both my children love to get involved and fold them with me.

 ## Samosas

1.

Fold

2.

Fold

3.

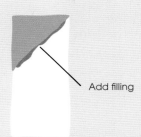

Add filling

4.

Fold and paste

5.

Fold and paste

6.

Spring rolls

1.

2.

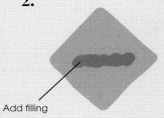

Add filling

3.

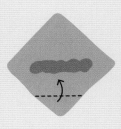

Fold

4.

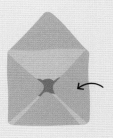

Fold

5.

Flour paste

Roll over

6.

Fold

Parathas

1.

Filling

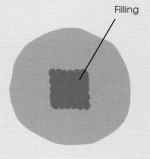

2.

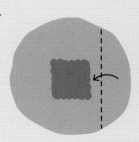

Fold

3.

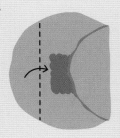

Fold

4.

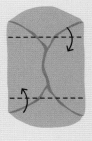

Fold

5.

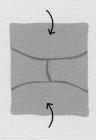

Fold

Peri-Peri Chicken Puff Pastries

Prep 30 minutes
Cook 1 hr

Peri-peri chicken pastries are ideal for batch cooking during Ramadan. With succulent marinated chicken and flaky, buttery pastry, this delightful snack disappears so quickly. From your first bite, you'll be left with a lasting impression.

Ingredients

2 tablespoons oil, plus extra for frying
1 onion, finely diced
500g chicken breasts, cut into large chunks
1 large potato, peeled and cut into 1cm cubes
30g unsalted butter
1 teaspoon ginger paste
1 teaspoon garlic paste
1 teaspoon green chilli paste
3 tablespoons red pepper, diced small
5 tablespoons tinned sweetcorn, drained
2 tablespoons peri-peri sauce
2 tablespoons tomato ketchup
2 tablespoons sweet chilli sauce
1 tablespoon peri-peri seasoning
1 tablespoon Kashmiri chilli powder
1 teaspoon ground black pepper
2 tablespoons finely chopped spring onion
5g fresh coriander, finely chopped
150g medium Cheddar cheese, grated
salt, to taste

PUFF PASTRIES

2 tablespoons plain flour, plus extra for dusting
2 x 320g packets of ready-rolled puff pastry
1 egg, beaten
sesame or nigella seeds, for sprinkling

Method

Heat the oil in a wok on a medium heat. Add the onions and fry until soft and translucent. Then add the chicken chunks, cover, and cook for 25 minutes, until the liquid released from the chicken has evaporated. Remove the chicken from the wok and place in a small bowl. Once the chicken has cooled, shred the chicken, pulling it apart using 2 forks or your fingers.

Meanwhile, cook the potatoes in salted boiling water for 8–10 minutes until only just tender, then drain in a colander and set aside.

In the same wok, gently melt the butter and add the ginger and garlic paste, chilli paste, red peppers, sweetcorn, potatoes, peri-peri sauce, tomato ketchup, sweet chilli sauce, peri-peri seasoning, Kashmiri chilli powder, black pepper, salt and the shredded chicken. Mix everything together and cook on a low heat for 3–4 minutes. Set aside to cool.

When cool, add the spring onions, coriander and grated cheese and mix together.

Make a flour paste by mixing the flour and 4 tablespoons of water in a small bowl to a smooth consistency. Preheat the oven to 190°C (gas mark 5) and line a baking sheet with baking paper.

Unroll the puff pastry sheets on a floured surface and cut out fifteen 10cm squares. Brush the edges of the squares with flour paste and place a heaped tablespoon of the chicken mixture in the middle of each. Fold the pastry squares into triangles or rectangles – whichever shape you prefer – enclosing the filling and pressing the edges together to seal the parcels. Cut 2 small slits in the tops of the parcels to allow hot air to escape while they are baking. Place the pastries on the prepared baking sheet, brush with beaten egg and sprinkle with sesame or nigella seeds. Cook for 25 minutes until golden brown. They are best eaten fresh on the day they are baked.

Spicy Vegetable Samosas

MAKES
25–30

Prep 30 minutes
Cook 15 minutes

· · · · ·✦· · · · · · · ·✦· · · · · · · ·✦· · · · · · · ·✦· · · · · ·✦· · · · ·

Every Ramadan, my mum would prepare a batch of vegetable samosas for those days when we felt like having a meat-free savoury snack. With a spicy mixed vegetable filling, wrapped in a triangle-shaped pastry, vegetable samosas are popular with everyone, and a perfect side dish to Chickpea Chaat (see page 115). These can be deep-fried or air-fried for a healthier option. Serve with sweet chilli sauce and a squeeze of fresh lemon juice, if desired.

Ingredients

1 medium potato, peeled and diced into 1cm pieces

2 tablespoons sunflower oil, plus extra for deep-frying

250g frozen mixed vegetables

1 onion, diced

1 teaspoon garlic paste

2 bird's-eye chillies, finely chopped

1 teaspoon chilli powder

1 teaspoon ground cumin

1 teaspoon ground coriander

½ teaspoon garam masala

5g fresh coriander, finely chopped

2 spring onions, finely chopped

2 tablespoons plain flour

25–30 samosa leaves

salt, to taste

Method

Parboil the potatoes in a saucepan of boiling water for 8–10 minutes until tender.

Meanwhile, heat 2 tablespoons of oil in a wok over a medium heat. Add the frozen mixed vegetables, onions, garlic paste, fresh chillies, chilli powder, ground cumin, ground coriander and salt. Cover and cook for 8–10 minutes until the vegetables have softened.

Drain the potato and add to the wok. Cook for 3 minutes, then remove from the heat. Set aside to cool. Once cooled, sprinkle over the garam masala, chopped coriander and spring onions.

Make a flour paste by mixing the flour and 4 tablespoons of water in a small bowl to a smooth consistency.

Lay a samosa leaf on a work surface with a short end facing you and fold to form a triangular pocket. See page 32 for how to do this. Fill the pocket with 1 heaped teaspoon of filling, then use a pastry brush to brush some of the flour paste on the top of the filled triangle. Continue to wrap the samosa, brushing paste between the layers to make a neat triangular parcel. Repeat with the remaining samosa leaves and filling.

Pour the oil for deep-frying into a large pan over a medium-high heat until it reaches 180°C. Fry the samosas in batches for 1–2 minutes on each side until golden. Drain on kitchen paper.

Puri with Mango Pulp

Prep 30 minutes
Cook 5 minutes

MAKES
16

Fresh, golden puffed puri with luscious, sweet, velvety mango pulp is the perfect combination. Puri dipped in mango is just heaven, with a taste of summer in every bite.

Ingredients

120g self-raising flour, plus extra for rolling
120g wholemeal chapati flour
1 teaspoon baking powder
2 tablespoons butter
2 tablespoons plain yogurt
1 tablespoon granulated sugar
60ml water
60ml milk
tinned mango pulp

Method

In a large bowl, combine the self-raising flour, chapati flour, baking powder, butter, yogurt and sugar, and use your fingertips to combine.

In a small pan, boil the water and milk over a low heat. Pour into the flour mixture slowly, kneading with your hands for 3–4 minutes until a soft dough is formed.

Divide the dough into 4 balls. Roll one of the balls in a little flour and flatten it a little with your hands. Use a rolling pin to roll it out on a lightly floured surface into a circle about 15–18cm in diameter and 3mm thick. Repeat with the other balls of dough.

Cut each circle into 4 triangles, so in total you will have 16 triangles.

Heat the oil for deep-frying in a large pan until it reaches 180°C. Fry the puris in the hot oil one by one so they have space to puff up. Puris fry very quickly, so when one side starts to puff up and turn golden, flip the puri over and fry until the other side is golden. Drain in a colander. They are best eaten fresh on the day they are fried, served with a bowl of mango pulp for dipping.

 TIP For fresh mango pulp, peel and cut the mango into chunks, then blitz the flesh in a blender. Simple as that.

Gulgulas, Drop Doughnuts

Prep 15 minutes
Cook 5 minutes

I remember helping my grandmother and mum make gulgulas (I call them sweet bhajiyas) –bite-sized drop doughnuts with an Indian twist. The batter is delicately spiced with aromatic cardamom and crushed fennel seeds, with the perfect balance of sweetness, lovingly fried to perfection until golden and crisp on the outside while remaining soft, pillowy and oh-so-fluffy on the inside.

Ingredients

180g plain flour
1 teaspoon crushed fennel seeds
1 teaspoon cardamom powder
1½ tablespoons ghee or clarified butter
60g caster sugar
1 teaspoon baking powder
1 egg, beaten
125ml full-fat milk
oil, for deep-frying
icing sugar, for dusting

Method

Place the flour, fennel seeds and cardamom powder in a large bowl, and use your fingertips to rub in the ghee. Add the sugar, baking powder, egg and milk and combine until the batter is smooth and thick. If the mixture is too thick, add a little more milk.

Heat the oil for deep-frying in a large saucepan until it reaches 180°C. Drop a little batter into the oil – if it sizzles, the oil is ready.

I use my hands to scoop up the batter, about a tablespoon at a time. Shape it into a ball and drop the batter carefully into the oil. Alternatively, shape the batter using two tablespoons. One to scoop the batter up and the other to push the batter off the first spoon. Do this in batches and do not overcrowd the pan. Fry for 1–2 minutes, turning occasionally so that the gulgulas are golden brown all over and soft and spongy on the inside. Use a slotted spoon to remove the gulgulas from the oil and place them onto kitchen paper to drain off the excess oil.

Leave to cool slightly, then dust with icing sugar and serve.

 TIP Add sliced banana to the batter to elevate these to the next level, and serve them with a chocolate dip.

MAKE IT

Healthier

If you're trying to make healthy choices without compromising on taste, look no further. Here are some satisfying, flavourful and delicious meals and treats for you and your family to enjoy, while embracing a healthier and more fulfilling lifestyle.

Breakfast Banana & Date Muffins

MAKES
12

Prep 15 minutes
Cook 20 minutes

These healthy muffins are simple to make and loaded with fruit. Perfect for a make-ahead breakfast, dessert or mid-morning snack, you'll want to have these on hand all the time!

Ingredients

100g reduced-fat margarine, at room temperature

100g light brown sugar

2 eggs, beaten

30g chopped pecans

30g chopped dates

30g rolled oats, plus extra for sprinkling

20g sunflower seeds, plus extra for sprinkling

1 teaspoon cinnamon

2 ripe bananas, mashed

200g self-raising flour

1 teaspoon baking powder

Method

Preheat the oven to 160°C (gas mark 3). Prepare a 12-hole muffin tin with muffin cases.

Cream the margarine and sugar together using an electric hand whisk until light and creamy. Whisk in the eggs one at a time until well incorporated. Add the pecans, dates, oats, sunflower seeds, cinnamon and bananas and mix everything together with a wooden spoon.

Sift the flour and baking powder into the mixture and slowly fold in. Do not over mix at this stage, as this can affect the texture of the muffins and make them dense. Using an ice cream scoop, divide the batter between the 12 muffin cases. Sprinkle the tops of the muffins with oats and sunflower seeds.

Bake for 20 minutes, until lightly golden. Check the muffins are baked by inserting a skewer into the centre, which should come out clean. Leave to cool. The muffins will keep for up to a week in an airtight container.

 Substitute the dates for blueberries to add a fruity twist.

Spiced Chicken Pittas

Prep 10 minutes
Cook 20 minutes

MAKES
4

This has to be the easiest and tastiest chicken mince filling. Ras el hanout, a fragrant and aromatic spice blend used in Middle Eastern cuisine, is the key ingredient. I absolutely love this spice – it will take your chicken, vegetable and fish dishes to another level and allow you to enjoy the rich and warm taste of the Middle East right in your own kitchen.

Ingredients

500g chicken mince
1 tablespoon ras el hanout
1 teaspoon ginger paste
1 teaspoon garlic paste
1 teaspoon ground black pepper
1 teaspoon chilli powder
1 tablespoon olive oil
1 red onion, finely diced
3 tablespoons diced red pepper
5g fresh parsley, chopped
4 pitta breads
4 lettuce leaves, chopped
2 fresh tomatoes, sliced
salt, to taste

Method

Place the mince, ras el hanout, ginger and garlic paste, black pepper, chilli powder and salt in a bowl and mix together.

Heat the oil in a medium pan on a medium heat. Add the mince mixture and break up any lumps. Stir in the red onion and red pepper, cover and cook for 20 minutes, stirring occasionally, until no moisture is left.

Sprinkle over the fresh parsley, then fill the pittas with the mince, lettuce and tomatoes.

Lemon, Chilli & Herb Cod Parcels

Prep 15 minutes
Cook 20 minutes

Baking fish in a parcel is such a fancy way of presenting it to your dinner guests. It's also a great way to seal in all the goodness, so as the fish bakes, it steams in its own juices, resulting in flaky, tender and moist fish. The fish pairs perfectly with couscous or baby potatoes.

Ingredients

3 lemons – 1 juiced, 1 thinly sliced and 1 cut into wedges
2 fresh red chillies, finely chopped
3 garlic cloves, crushed
1 teaspoon ground black pepper
5g fresh dill, chopped, plus extra for garnish
5g fresh parsley, chopped
2 x 150g skinless cod loin
2 tablespoons olive oil
salt, to taste

VEGETABLES

2 tablespoons Kalamata olives, halved
150g baby tomatoes, halved
150g tenderstem broccoli
150g green beans, trimmed and halved
1 tablespoon olive oil
1 teaspoon dried oregano
1 teaspoon ground black pepper

Method

Preheat the oven to 180°C (gas mark 4). Cut out 2 pieces of parchment paper, 25 x 35cm, for your parcels.

Put the lemon juice, chillies, garlic, black pepper, dill, parsley, olive oil and salt in a bowl and mix together. Add the cod loins and coat in the marinade.

For the vegetables, toss the olives, tomatoes, broccoli, green beans, olive oil, dried oregano and black pepper in a bowl, and season with salt. Divide the vegetables between the 2 pieces of parchment and place the cod loins on top. Place lemon slices on top of each cod loin.

Scrunch up the edges of the baking paper to seal the fish and vegetable into a parcel. Place the parcels on a baking sheet and cover each one separately with foil; this helps to keep the steam and juices locked in.

Bake for 20 minutes until the fish is flaky and opaque. If the loins are quite thick, they may need slightly longer. Remove the foil, place the parcels onto a serving plate, open slightly and garnish with dill and lemon wedges.

 You can use salmon or halibut in place of cod – they both taste just as good!

 You can also add some trimmed asparagus to the parcels.

Grilled Chipotle Chicken Skewers

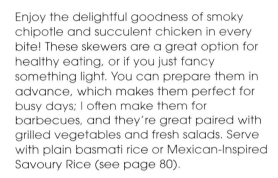

MAKES
6-7

Prep 15 minutes
Cook 30 minutes

Enjoy the delightful goodness of smoky chipotle and succulent chicken in every bite! These skewers are a great option for healthy eating, or if you just fancy something light. You can prepare them in advance, which makes them perfect for busy days; I often make them for barbecues, and they're great paired with grilled vegetables and fresh salads. Serve with plain basmati rice or Mexican-Inspired Savoury Rice (see page 80).

Ingredients

500g chicken breast, cut into bite-sized chunks

2 tablespoons chipotle chilli powder

2 tablespoons honey

1 teaspoon garlic paste

1 teaspoon ground black pepper

1 red onion, cut into 2–3cm chunks

1 red pepper, cut into 2–3cm chunks

1 green pepper, cut into 2–3cm chunks

3 tablespoons chipotle sauce

2 tablespoons olive oil

salt, to taste

Method

Soak 6–7 wooden skewers in water to prevent them from burning. Preheat the oven to 190°C (gas mark 5) and line a baking tray with foil or baking paper.

Place the chicken pieces in a bowl with the chipotle chilli powder, honey, garlic and black pepper, and mix together.

Thread pieces of chicken, red onion and peppers onto the wooden skewers, alternating between each one until they are all used up. Place the skewers on the tray, brush with chipotle sauce and drizzle with olive oil.

Bake for 30 minutes, turning the skewers halfway through.

Creamy Cabbage Corn Slaw

Prep 20 minutes

This wonderful creamy cabbage and corn slaw is a mix of textures and flavours and the perfect accompaniment for fish and grilled meats. I also use this as a topping for jacket potatoes or as a sandwich filler.

Ingredients

½ red cabbage, finely shredded
1 red onion, finely sliced
1 carrot, julienned
200g tin of sweetcorn, drained
1 teaspoon dried oregano
1 teaspoon ground black pepper
250g reduced-fat mayonnaise
2 spring onions, finely chopped
5g fresh parsley, finely chopped
salt, to taste

Method

Place the red cabbage, red onion, carrot, sweetcorn, oregano, pepper and salt in a large bowl. Add the mayonnaise and stir until everything is mixed together nicely.

Garnish with spring onions and parsley, and serve.

 You can also use white cabbage for this dish, or a mixture of the two.

 To make the dish spicy, add some chopped jalapeño chillies and a little chilli powder.

Air-Fried Peri-Peri Chicken with Wedges

SERVES
2-3

Prep 40 minutes
Cook 35 minutes

My family loves peri-peri chicken. Juicy, tender, succulent chicken is super easy to make in your air-fryer and will be on your plate in no time at all. The air-fried wedges are crisp on the outside and fluffy on the inside, and both are perfect served alongside Creamy Cabbage Corn Slaw (see page 50) and a side salad.

Ingredients

4 chicken breasts or thighs
2 tablespoons olive oil
2 tablespoons peri-peri seasoning
1 tablespoon dried parsley
1 tablespoon ground black pepper
1 tablespoon chilli powder
1 tablespoon peri-peri sauce
1 teaspoon ground turmeric
1 teaspoon onion powder
1 teaspoon garlic granules
2 tablespoons lemon juice
salt, to taste

WEDGES

3 large potatoes, such as King Edward, Maris Piper or Russet, skin on, cut into wedges
1 tablespoon olive oil
1 teaspoon ground black pepper
1 teaspoon garlic powder
1 teaspoon cayenne pepper
salt, to taste

Method

Cut a few slits into the flesh of the chicken pieces, then place them into a bowl and add the remaining ingredients. Mix well and coat the chicken thoroughly, rubbing the spices into the slits. Set aside in the fridge to marinate for 30 minutes.

Preheat the air-fryer to 180°C. You could also line the basket with baking paper, if desired, to save on the washing up!

Place the chicken in the air-fryer, but do not overcrowd the basket. You need to make sure there is space for air to circulate, which will ensure the chicken is cooked evenly. The chicken should take about 20 minutes to cook, and the internal temperature should be 75°C. If you have a thermometer attached to your air-fryer, this makes it so much easier to make sure the chicken is at the right temperature, resulting in perfectly cooked, juicy meat. For the wedges, parboil the potatoes for 15 minutes in a pot of salted boiling water. Drain, then drizzle over the oil and season with salt, pepper, garlic powder and cayenne pepper. Toss everything together well and air-fry at 180°C for 12 minutes until the edges are crisp and golden.

'Use-It-Up' Pasta

Prep 15 minutes
Cook 30 minutes

SERVES
3–4

We always have leftover vegetables at home, and I don't like anything going to waste, so what better way to use them up than in this veggie pasta. It's so versatile, and you can use whatever leftover veg you have on hand. You can also use any pasta you like. So this is the basic recipe, but feel free to mix it up!

Ingredients

300g pasta of your choice

1 teaspoon olive oil, plus extra if needed

1 teaspoon garlic paste

1 carrot, cut into small chunks

400g tin chopped tomatoes

200g tin sweetcorn, drained, or use frozen sweetcorn

½ red pepper, cut into small chunks

½ green pepper, cut into small chunks

½ teaspoon chilli flakes

½ teaspoon dried Italian seasoning, or other dried herbs of your choice

½ teaspoon ground black pepper

150g grated mozzarella cheese, optional

salt, to taste

Method

Cook the pasta in a pot of boiling salted water according to the packet instructions. You can add a little oil to the water, if desired, to prevent the pasta from sticking. Drain in a colander, but retain about 120ml of the pasta water. This will be used to keep the pasta from drying out.

Meanwhile, in another large pot, add the oil and garlic paste and cook on a low heat for about 30 seconds, until fragrant. Add the carrots, cover, and cook for 6–7 minutes until they soften a little.

Blitz the chopped tomatoes in a food processor and stir into the carrots along with the sweetcorn, peppers, chilli flakes, Italian seasoning, black pepper and salt. Give it all a mix, cover, and cook until the tomatoes have reduced, about 15 minutes.

Add the pasta and reserved pasta water and stir gently, making sure you don't break the pasta, then cover and cook for 4–5 minutes until the pasta's warmed through nicely. At this point, you can sprinkle over grated cheese if you like your pasta cheesy.

Chilli Chicken & Mango Salad

MAKES
4

Prep 15 minutes
Cook 12 minutes

Salads are incredibly versatile, refreshing, colourful and nutritious, and a fantastic choice when you want something quick and healthy. In my home, a variety of different salads are on the menu a few times a week, especially during Ramadan when you want something light for iftar. I love the sweet and spicy fusion of flavours in this dish – the sweetness of the mango complements the fiery kick of the chilli, making this salad perfect for summer days.

Ingredients

1 teaspoon garlic granules
1 teaspoon onion granules
1 teaspoon chilli flakes
1 fresh red chilli, finely sliced
1 teaspoon paprika
1 teaspoon ground black pepper
2 chicken breasts
low-calorie cooking spray
100g Romaine lettuce, sliced
30g baby spinach
1 red onion, finely sliced
50g radishes, sliced
150g cherry tomatoes, halved
2 ripe mangoes, peeled, and flesh cut into cubes
juice of 1 lime
3g fresh coriander, finely chopped
salt, to taste

Method

In a bowl, mix together the garlic granules, onion granules, chilli flakes, red chilli, paprika, black pepper and salt. Slice the chicken breasts in half horizontally and coat the chicken in the spices.

Spray a frying pan or griddle pan with low-calorie cooking spray and set on a medium heat. Add the chicken breasts, cover and cook for about 10 minutes, turning the chicken halfway through, until cooked through.

Arrange the lettuce, baby spinach, onions, radishes, tomatoes and cubed mangoes on a large platter. Slice the chicken thinly and arrange on top of the salad. Squeeze over some lime juice and scatter over the coriander.

 Add pomegranate seeds for that extra crunch, and serve with fresh strawberries for added sweetness and a pop of colour.

Beef Mince Cottage Pie

SERVES
4

Prep 20 minutes
Cook 1 hour 10 minutes

Cottage pie is a classic heart-warming dish. Tender and succulent meat and veg in a luscious gravy that binds everything together, topped with a layer of creamy, melt-in-your-mouth mash. This recipes uses lean mince making this classic meal healthier for the whole family to enjoy any time.

Ingredients

low-calorie cooking spray

1 large onion, finely diced

2 garlic cloves, crushed

500g beef mince (5% fat or less)

2 carrots, cut into small chunks

100g frozen peas

1 tablespoon Worcestershire sauce

1 teaspoon chilli powder

½ teaspoon hot paprika

½ teaspoon dried mixed herbs

½ teaspoon ground black pepper, plus extra for the mash, to taste

2 tablespoons tomato purée

350ml vegetable stock, made with 2 vegetable stock cubes

600g potatoes, peeled and cut into 2.5cm chunks

5g fresh parsley, finely chopped

salt, to taste

 TIP Make sure the mince mixture is cool before topping with the mashed potato, otherwise the mash may sink through the mince.

Method

Preheat the oven to 190°C (gas mark 5). Heat a large pan on a medium heat and spray with low-calorie cooking spray. Add the onions and fry for 10 minutes until soft and translucent. Add the garlic and fry until fragrant, then add the mince and cook for about 5 minutes, until browned, stirring occasionally and breaking up any lumps.

Add the carrots, peas, Worcestershire sauce, chilli powder, hot paprika, dried mixed herbs, salt and black pepper, cover, and cook for 15 minutes until the water released from the mince has evaporated.

Stir the tomato purée into the stock, then pour this mixture into the pot, stir, and simmer on a low heat for 15 minutes until the mixture starts to thicken.

Meanwhile, boil the potatoes in a pot of salted boiling water until tender. Drain and mash well, season with salt and black pepper, and set aside.

Pour the mince mixture into a shallow ovenproof dish and leave to cool for 10 minutes before topping with the mash. Level the top evenly using a fork.

Bake for 30 minutes until golden brown on top. Garnish with fresh parsley.

 TIP Cottage pie is a great dish to prepare a day in advance – just leave it in the fridge and heat it up when you're ready.

Black-Eyed Beans & Spinach

SERVES 4

Prep 15 minutes
Cook 35 minutes

This curry is one of my favourite vegetarian dishes. Packed with essential nutrients in the form of black-eyed beans and tender spinach, it's so tasty and delicious, a balanced and wholesome meal that doesn't require a lot of oil, making it perfect for health-conscious people. I like to serve with fresh chapati.

Ingredients

2 tablespoons sunflower oil

2 onions, finely diced

1 tomato, finely chopped

5 tablespoons tinned chopped tomatoes

1 teaspoon garlic paste

1 teaspoon chilli powder

1 teaspoon ground cumin

1 teaspoon ground coriander

½ teaspoon ground turmeric

2 x 400g tins black-eyed beans, drained and rinsed

500g spinach, finely chopped

pinch of garam masala

5g fresh coriander, finely chopped

1 lemon

salt, to taste

Method

Heat the oil in a large pan on a medium heat, add the onions and fry until golden brown, about 15 minutes. Add the fresh tomatoes, tinned tomatoes, garlic paste, chilli powder, ground cumin, ground coriander, ground turmeric and salt, and cook for 10 minutes, or until the tomatoes have reduced and softened.

Stir in the black-eyed beans and chopped spinach, cover, and cook for 5 minutes. Pour in 150ml water and simmer on a low heat for 5 minutes until the curry has thickened slightly.

Finish with a sprinkling of garam masala, chopped fresh coriander and a squeeze of lemon juice.

 TIP You can use dried beans in this recipe. Just soak them overnight, as they cook faster than beans that have not been soaked. Dried beans will take longer to cook than tinned beans, so check the package for instructions.

Anisa's Spaghetti Bolognese

SERVES
4–5

Prep 25 minutes
Cook 50 minutes

Spag bol with an Indian and healthier twist! This timeless classic is made with very little oil and succulent lean lamb mince and vegetables, flavoured with aromatic Indian spices and Italian herbs in a savoury-sweet, slightly tangy tomato sauce that goes perfectly with al dente spaghetti. Proper comfort food without the guilt, and a low-fat meal for your whole family to enjoy!

Ingredients

low-calorie cooking spray
1 large onion, finely diced
1 tablespoon garlic paste
500g lamb mince
1 carrot, peeled and cut into small chunks
1 tablespoon Worcestershire sauce
1 courgette, cut into small chunks
½ red pepper, cut into small chunks
½ green pepper, cut into small chunks
1 teaspoon chilli powder
1 teaspoon ground cumin
1 teaspoon ground coriander
½ teaspoon dried oregano
½ teaspoon ground black pepper
300g tinned chopped tomatoes
400g dried spaghetti
5g fresh parsley, finely chopped
salt, to taste

Method

Preheat a wok on a low heat and spray with low-calorie cooking oil. Add the onions and cook for 5 minutes until the onions have softened.

Add the garlic paste, mince, carrots and Worcestershire sauce. Mix to combine, cover with a lid, and cook on a medium heat for 25 minutes until the liquid evaporates.

Stir in the courgettes, red and green peppers, chilli powder, ground cumin, ground coriander, oregano, black pepper and salt. Mix everything together, cover, and cook for 4–5 minutes, until the courgettes and peppers have softened but still have a bite to them.

Blitz the tinned tomatoes in a food processor and add to the mince. Cover and cook for 8–10 minutes on a low heat. The Bolognese will start to thicken slightly.

Bring a large pan of salted water to the boil. Add the spaghetti and cook as per the packet instructions, then drain in a colander.

Divide the spaghetti between serving bowls, top with the Bolognese sauce and sprinkle with parsley.

Lamb Kebab with Mint Dip

MAKES
20

Prep 25 minutes
Cook 12 minutes

Deliciously juicy lamb kebabs are perfect for any get-together or family day trip. My children love them, especially with puri (see page 37). Using the puri as a wrap, place a kebab in the centre, add a dollop of fresh mint dip, and each mouthful will leave you craving another.

Ingredients

500g lamb mince
1 large onion, finely diced
1 tablespoon ground coriander
1 tablespoon ground cumin
1 teaspoon chilli powder
1 teaspoon ground black pepper
100g shop-bought panko breadcrumbs
5 fresh green chillies
5 garlic cloves
5cm piece fresh root ginger, peeled
5g fresh mint leaves, finely chopped
5g fresh coriander, finely chopped
oil, for cooking and greasing
salt, to taste

MINT DIP
10g fresh mint leaves
200g Greek yogurt
½ teaspoon ground black pepper
pinch of salt

Method

In a large bowl, add the mince, onion, ground coriander, ground cumin, chilli powder, pepper, breadcrumbs and salt.

Using a pestle and mortar, crush the green chillies, garlic cloves and ginger to a paste, and add this to the mince mixture. Sprinkle over the mint and coriander and mix everything together with your hands.

Rub a little oil into the palms of your hands to prevent sticking, then take about 2 tablespoons of the mixture and form it into a patty shape. Repeat with the remaining mixture.

If you have an air fryer, working in batches place the patties in your air fryer making sure not to overcrowd the drawer. Spray with a little oil. Cook at 180°C for 10–12 minutes. Alternatively, you can cook them in the oven by placing the patties on a baking sheet lined with parchment paper, spraying them with a little oil and baking at 190°C for 30 minutes. The patties are ready when they have shrunk slightly and are golden on the outside.

To make the mint dip, blitz the mint in a food processor and stir into the Greek yogurt. Season with the pepper and salt and serve alongside the lamb kebabs.

Burji, Spicy Scrambled Eggs

Prep 15 minutes
Cook 35 minutes

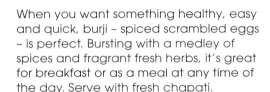

When you want something healthy, easy and quick, burji – spiced scrambled eggs – is perfect. Bursting with a medley of spices and fragrant fresh herbs, it's great for breakfast or as a meal at any time of the day. Serve with fresh chapati.

Ingredients

2 tablespoons sunflower oil
2 large onions, finely sliced
2 large potatoes, cut into small chunks
1 teaspoon garlic paste
1 teaspoon chilli paste
1 teaspoon ground cumin
1 teaspoon ground coriander
½ teaspoon ground turmeric
½ teaspoon chilli powder
100g fenugreek leaves, finely chopped
4 spring onions, finely chopped
6 eggs, beaten
salt, to taste
5g fresh coriander, finely chopped

Method

Heat the oil in a large pan on a medium heat, add the onions and fry until golden brown, about 15 minutes. Add the potatoes, cover, and cook for around 20 minutes until almost tender.

Add the garlic paste, chilli paste, ground cumin, ground coriander, ground turmeric, chilli powder, fenugreek leaves, spring onions and salt. Mix everything together, then add the eggs and start scrambling them by gently moving them across the pan using a wooden spoon. Cook for 4–5 minutes, stirring constantly to ensure they don't stick to the pan.

Garnish with chopped coriander.

 You could add red or green peppers to this dish – just sauté them along with the onions. You could also add frozen peas with the potatoes.

Masala Bhindi, Okra Masala

Prep 15 minutes
Cook 35 minutes

Bhindi masala, or bhindi fry, is one of the simplest vegetarian dishes you can make. Growing up, I remember my mum preparing this, as it's one of my dad's favourite meals. Like most children I wasn't a fan of veggies when I was younger, but as an adult I've realised how delicious it is and it's now a regular in my home. I think this dish is where my love for vegetarian food began. It might sound weird, but I love it with jam. Scoop a bit of jam with chapati and masala bhindi, it really is delicious – give it a try!

Ingredients

250g bhindi (okra)
1 teaspoon lemon juice
2 tablespoons sunflower oil
1 teaspoon garlic paste
½ teaspoon chilli paste
1 teaspoon ground cumin
1 teaspoon ground coriander
½ teaspoon ground turmeric
1 teaspoon chilli powder
1 tomato, finely chopped
2 tablespoons tinned chopped tomatoes
¼ teaspoon garam masala
3g fresh coriander, finely chopped
salt, to taste

Method

Wash the bhindi whole and dry them well. Chop off both ends and discard. Cut the bhindi into 1cm pieces.

Heat a medium wok over a medium-sized wok on a low heat and add the bhindi pieces and lemon juice. Dry-fry them first, uncovered, to remove any stickiness. This can take around 10 minutes.

Add the oil, garlic paste, chilli paste, ground cumin, ground coriander, ground turmeric, chilli powder, fresh tomato and chopped tomatoes and salt. Mix everything together, cover and cook for 25 minutes until the bhindi is tender.

Sprinkle over the garam masala and fresh coriander.

 Cooking bhindi without stir-frying first can make them slimy. Choose tender bhindi, as they cook faster, and avoid washing them after cutting, as moisture adds to the stickiness.

One Pot

WONDERS

When time is precious and energy is low,
especially during Ramadan, these hearty,
mouth-watering one-pot dishes are easy to
make and require minimal kitchen work, so you
can spend quality time with your loved ones.
From comforting and filling soups to aromatic
rice dishes that fill the air with an irresistible
aroma, these recipes are sure to become
your go-to favourites!

Mediterranean Chicken & Vegetables

SERVES
4

Prep 20 minutes
Cook 40 minutes

A delicious, easy and healthy dinner, bursting with flavour. This recipe combines the distinct flavours of Mediterranean seasonings with succulent juicy chicken breasts, thighs or drumsticks and vibrant fresh vegetables, roasted together in a single tray. Perfect for a weeknight dinner for the family.

Ingredients

1 red pepper, cut into 2.5cm chunks
1 green pepper, cut into 2.5cm chunks
1 courgette, cut into 2.5cm chunks
1 large red onion, cut into 2.5cm chunks
50g black olives, drained
8 chicken breasts, thighs or drumsticks
2 tablespoons olive oil
4 garlic cloves, crushed
2 teaspoons hot paprika
1 teaspoon dried oregano
2 teaspoons ground black pepper
1 lemon, zested and juiced
200g tomatoes, on the vine
salt, to taste

Method

Preheat the oven to 190°C (gas mark 5). Line a large roasting tin with foil.

Place the cut vegetables and black olives in a large mixing bowl. Add the chicken pieces, drizzle over the oil and add the crushed garlic, paprika, oregano, black pepper, lemon juice and zest and salt. Toss everything together well to combine, making sure the veggies and chicken pieces are evenly coated.

Transfer the chicken and vegetables to the roasting tin. Spread out well in a single layer and place the tomatoes on the vine on top.

Cover with foil and cook in the oven for 30–40 minutes, removing the foil halfway through. The chicken should be golden and thoroughly cooked, with the juices running clear. Serve with a side of leafy green salad.

 You could also add some parboiled baby potatoes and carrots with the cut vegetables to the dish.

Chicken Tikka Rice

Prep 40 minutes
Cook 1 hr

SERVES
5-6

This is my go-to one-pot meal, ideal for those days when you are rushing around and have no time to spare. Everything cooks together in a single pot, saving you time and effort. This mouth-watering dish brings together tender pieces of chicken cooked with authentic Indian spices and aromatic basmati rice, making it a delicious homemade feast.

Ingredients

350g basmati rice
4 tablespoons oil
2 large onions, finely diced
500g chicken breast, cut into bite-sized chunks
1 tablespoon ginger paste
1 tablespoon garlic paste
2 tablespoons chicken tikka masala paste
1 teaspoon ground turmeric
1 tablespoon ground cumin
1 tablespoon ground coriander
1 teaspoon chilli powder
1 teaspoon Kashmiri chilli powder
200g tomato passata
700ml water
5g fresh coriander, finely chopped
1 fresh lemon, cut into wedges
salt, to taste

WHOLE SPICES
½ teaspoon cumin seeds
2 cinnamon sticks
2 bay leaves
3 cardamom pods
3 cloves
3 black peppercorns
2 star anise

Method

Wash the rice in a sieve under cold running water until the water runs clear. Then soak in a bowl of cold water for 30 minutes. This will reduce the cooking time and help the rice cook evenly.

Heat a large pot on medium heat and pour in the oil. Add all the whole spices and fry for 30–40 seconds until they start to sizzle. Add the onions and fry gently until golden brown, about 15 minutes.

Add the chicken pieces, ginger and garlic paste, tikka masala paste, turmeric, cumin, coriander, the chilli powder and the Kashmiri chilli powder and cook for 20 minutes until no moisture is left from the chicken.

Stir in the tomato passata and cook for 8–10 minutes, until the sauce is reduced. Add the rice, pour in the water, season with salt, and stir. Partially cover the pan with a lid (not completely or the water may boil over) and cook for 15 minutes until the water has been absorbed, then give it a stir once without disturbing the rice too much. Cover with the lid fully and cook for another 15 minutes on a low heat – the build-up of steam will cook and fluff up the rice.

Serve on a large platter, garnished with chopped coriander and lemon wedges, with a glass of sweet yogurt lassi.

Paneer & Spinach Curry

Prep 20 minutes
Cook 45 minutes

SERVES
2–3

Paneer and spinach curry is a popular vegetarian dish – quick and easy to make and so comforting and tasty. Paneer is a type of cheese that pairs well with fresh spinach. The texture is soft but the cheese doesn't melt, which makes it a perfect addition to curries. Serve with warm fresh chapatis.

Ingredients

3 tablespoons sunflower oil
250g paneer, cut into bite-sized pieces
1 large onion, finely sliced
2 teaspoons garlic paste
1 vine tomato, cut into small pieces
1 tablespoon tomato purée
½ teaspoon chilli powder
1 teaspoon ground cumin
1 teaspoon ground coriander
½ teaspoon ground turmeric
450g spinach, finely chopped
salt, to taste

Method

Heat the oil in a large pan on a medium heat. Once hot, add the paneer and cook for 2–3 minutes until golden brown on all sides. Transfer to a plate and set aside.

In the same pan, fry the onions until golden brown, about 15 minutes. Add the garlic paste and cook until fragrant, then add the tomatoes, tomato purée, chilli powder, ground cumin, ground coriander, ground turmeric and salt and cook for 10 minutes until the tomatoes have softened and the spices have blended nicely.

Stir in the chopped spinach and about 3 tablespoons water to release all the flavours from the bottom of the pan. Cook for 12 minutes until the spinach has wilted.

Add the cooked paneer and warm through for 2–3 minutes.

Lamb Akhni

Prep 30 minutes
Cook 1 hr 50 minutes

SERVES
4-5

Akhni is a staple dish in our home – it's a one-pot curry and rice dish and very aromatic. Made with traditional fragrant spices, the meat is cooked until tender, then tomato passata is added to the masala, giving a thick, gravy-like base allowing the rice to absorb all the flavours.

Ingredients

1 teaspoon ground turmeric

2 tablespoons ground coriander

1 tablespoon ground cumin

1 tablespoon chilli powder

1 tablespoon Kashmiri chilli powder

1 tablespoon chilli paste

1 heaped tablespoon ginger paste

1 heaped tablespoon garlic paste

1kg mixed lamb meat, leg and shoulder pieces, diced into approximately 3.5cm chunks

125ml sunflower oil

3 large onions, finely sliced

400g tomato passata

700g basmati rice, rinsed until the water runs clear

1.6 litres water

10 baby potatoes, halved

2 jalapeños chillies, halved with seeds left in

5g fresh coriander, finely chopped, plus extra to garnish

½ tsp garam masala

1 lemon, cut into wedges, to serve

salt, to taste

WHOLE SPICES

5 cloves

5 black peppercorns

4 cardamom pods

2 bay leaves

2 cinnamon sticks

2 star anise

Method

Place the ground turmeric, ground coriander, ground cumin, chilli powder, Kashmiri chilli powder, chilli paste and ginger and garlic pastes in a bowl with the lamb and mix everything together well to coat the lamb pieces.

Heat a large pot on a low heat. Add the oil and whole spices and fry for 40 seconds until fragrant. Add the onions and fry until golden brown, this can take about 15 minutes.

Add the meat, cover, and cook on a medium heat for around 45 minutes, until the water has evaporated and the meat is tender. Make sure to stir the pot occasionally so the meat doesn't stick or burn.

Pour in the passata, stir, and cook for 10 minutes until the tomato has reduced and the spices are nicely blended.

Add the rice to the pot along with the water, potatoes, jalapeño chillies, fresh coriander and garam masala and stir everything together well. Partially cover with a lid so the water doesn't overboil, and cook on a medium heat for 15 minutes until the water has been absorbed, then stir once without disturbing the rice too much. Cover fully with the lid and cook for another 20 minutes on a low heat – the build-up of steam will cook and fluff up the rice.

Serve on a large platter, garnished with chopped coriander and lemon wedges.

Masala Prawns & Rice

Prep 20 minutes
Cook 45 minutes

I like to have a pack or two of prawns in my freezer, in preparation for those days when you're looking for a quick, fuss-free meal. I use raw king prawns, as they release their juices as they cook in the spices and rice, enhancing the overall taste of this dish. The masala is made with a perfect blend of Indian spices, rich, tangy tomatoes, fresh mint and coriander, and the tender, succulent prawns. The zing from the lemon is the final touch.

Ingredients

4 tablespoons oil

1 large onion, finely diced

1 tablespoon garlic paste

200g tinned chopped tomatoes

1 vine tomato

1 tablespoon ground coriander

1 tablespoon ground cumin

1 teaspoon chilli flakes

1 teaspoon ground turmeric

½ red pepper, cut into 2.5cm chunks

½ green pepper, cut into 2.5cm chunks

100g fresh or frozen garden peas

300g raw king prawns, cleaned and deveined

250g basmati rice

500ml water

5g fresh mint, finely chopped

5g fresh coriander, finely chopped, plus extra to garnish,

salt, to taste

juice of 1 lemon

Method

Heat the oil in a large pan on a medium heat. Sauté the onions and garlic paste until soft and fragrant, about 5–10 minutes.

Blitz the tinned tomatoes and chop the fresh tomato into small chunks, then add to the pan (using both fresh and tinned tomatoes adds texture and taste to the dish) along with the spices and stir to combine, about 8–10 minutes. The tomatoes will break down and reduce.

Add the red and green peppers, peas, prawns and rice to the pan, and stir gently to coat in the tomato masala. Pour in the water, add fresh mint and coriander, season with salt and give everything another stir.

Bring to a simmer and partially cover the pan with a lid (do not cover completely or the water may boil over). Cook on a medium heat for 10 minutes until the water has been absorbed, then give it another quick stir without disturbing the rice too much.

Cover with the lid fully and cook for 15 minutes on a low heat – the build-up of steam will cook and fluff up the rice, and the prawns will steam with the rice, so they will be juicy and tender. Serve on a platter, garnished with coriander and a squeeze of fresh lemon juice. Delicious!

Moroccan Harira Soup

Prep 20 minutes
Cook 1 hr 20 minutes

Hearty and comforting, this Moroccan harira soup contains tender pieces of lamb delicately spiced with cumin, ginger, saffron and cinnamon, enriched with a blend of tomatoes, lentils and chickpeas. As the pot simmers, your kitchen will be filled with a flavourful aroma.

Ingredients

2 tablespoons olive oil

2 bay leaves

1 onion, finely diced

400g boneless lamb, cut into small pieces

2 teaspoons garlic paste

1 fresh red chilli, finely chopped

½ teaspoon ground cinnamon

1 teaspoon chilli powder

1 teaspoon ground cumin

1 teaspoon ground ginger

1 teaspoon ground black pepper

1 teaspoon saffron threads

150g red lentils

1 tablespoon tomato purée

400g tin of chopped tomatoes

1.5 litres water

100g rice, or use broken vermicelli pasta, if preferred

400g tin of chickpeas, drained

2 carrots, peeled and cut into small chunks

5g fresh coriander, finely chopped

5g fresh parsley, finely chopped

1 fresh lemon

salt, to taste

Method

Heat the oil in a large pot on a medium heat. Add the bay leaves and onions and cook until the onions have softened. Add the lamb pieces along with the garlic paste, mix to combine, then cover and cook until the water released from the lamb has evaporated, about 30 minutes.

Add the fresh red chilli, spices, red lentils, tomato purée, tinned tomatoes and salt. Stir, and cook for 5 minutes so the spices are incorporated nicely.

Pour over the water and rice or vermicelli pasta, add the carrots, bring to the boil, then reduce the heat and simmer for 30 minutes. After 30 minutes, add the chickpeas and simmer for another 15 minutes.

Serve in individual soup bowls, topped with the fresh herbs and a squeeze of fresh lemon juice.

 To thicken the soup slightly, add 2 tablespoons of cornflour to 120ml water, mix to a smooth paste, stir into the soup and simmer for 4–5 minutes.

Chicken & Sweetcorn Soup

SERVES
4

Prep 20 minutes
Cook 50 minutes

This quick and easy soup is made with simple store-cupboard ingredients. My children love it with garlic bread served alongside. Although it's great at any time of the year, it's especially good during the winter months, and makes a delicious starter when you have guests round.

Ingredients

50g unsalted butter

1 onion, diced

400g chicken breast, cut into small pieces

1 teaspoon garlic paste

½ teaspoon ground black pepper

1 x 400g tin cream-style sweetcorn

1 potato, cut into small chunks

1 carrot, cut into small chunks

½ teaspoon ground cumin

½ teaspoon chilli flakes

3 tablespoons milk

1 heaped tablespoon cornflour

1.5 litres chicken stock, made with 2 chicken stock cubes

50g spaghetti, broken into 2.5cm pieces

5g fresh parsley, finely chopped

salt, to taste

Method

Heat the butter in a large pot on a low heat until melted, then add the onion and fry until soft and translucent, about 15 minutes. Add the chicken pieces, garlic paste, black pepper and salt, increase the heat to medium, and cook for about 20 minutes, until the water released from the chicken has evaporated.

Add the sweetcorn, potatoes, carrots, ground cumin and chilli flakes, mix everything together, and cook for 5 minutes so the spices blend in nicely.

Stir the milk and cornflour together in a small bowl.

Pour the stock into the pot of chicken and sweetcorn, add the spaghetti and stir through the cornflour slurry. Simmer on a low heat for 25 minutes until the soup starts to thicken slightly.

Sprinkle with chopped fresh parsley and serve.

Easy Dhal

Prep 25 minutes
Cook 1 hour

- - · · · · ✦ · · · · ✦ · · · · ✦ · · · · ✦ · · · · ✦ · · · · ✦

This humble dhal has been part of my life for as long as I can remember. It's proper soul food. I remember my mum preparing a pot along with fresh chapatis, and my dad would make a very simple but delicious condiment of finely sliced red onion and malt vinegar to go with it. So if you want something light for lunch or dinner, this dhal is perfect for you.

Ingredients

250g moong dhal (split yellow lentils), rinsed until the water runs clear

2 tablespoons ghee or sunflower oil

½ teaspoon cumin seeds

5 curry leaves

1 large onion, finely diced

1 large vine tomato

1 teaspoon garlic paste

1 teaspoon ginger paste

1 teaspoon ground cumin

1 teaspoon ground coriander

½ teaspoon ground turmeric

1 teaspoon chilli powder or chilli paste

¼ teaspoon garam masala

salt, to taste

3g fresh coriander, finely chopped

1 lemon

Method

Boil the dhal in 800ml cold, salted water and bring to the boil on a medium heat. Skim off any white froth that forms on top while the dhal is simmering. Partially cover with a lid so the water doesn't boil over, then reduce the heat to a gentle simmer and cook for 25 minutes until the lentils have softened. Remove from the heat and transfer the dhal to a bowl.

In the same pot, add the ghee or oil, cumin seeds and curry leaves and fry until fragrant. Add the onions and sauté until soft and translucent, about 10 minutes.

With a knife, score an X in the base of the tomato and submerge it in a bowl of hot water for about 1 minute; the skin will start to loosen and peel away easily. Finely dice the tomato and add to the pot along with the garlic and ginger pastes, ground cumin, ground coriander, ground turmeric and chilli powder or paste. Cook for 20 minutes until the tomatoes have softened.

Stir in the boiled dhal, sprinkle over the garam masala and finish with chopped coriander and a squeeze of lemon juice.

 Vine tomatoes are sweet, juicy and extremely aromatic, and add texture and freshness to your dish.

Chana Batata, Chickpea & Potato Masala

SERVES
4–5

Prep 15 minutes
Cook 30 minutes

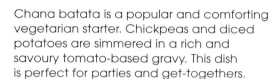

Chana batata is a popular and comforting vegetarian starter. Chickpeas and diced potatoes are simmered in a rich and savoury tomato-based gravy. This dish is perfect for parties and get-togethers.

Ingredients

1 teaspoon mustard seeds

2 tablespoons oil

8–9 curry leaves

300g tomato passata

1 teaspoon garlic paste

1 1/2 teaspoons chilli powder

1/2 teaspoon ground turmeric

1 teaspoon hot paprika

1 teaspoon ground cumin

1 teaspoon ground coriander

3 tablespoons tamarind sauce

3 tablespoons chilli sauce

2 tablespoons jaggery or granulated sugar

200g tin of sweetcorn, drained

400g tin of kala chana
(brown chickpeas), drained

400g tin of chickpeas, drained

300g tinned baby potatoes, drained and halved

240ml water

salt, to taste

5g fresh coriander, finely chopped, to garnish

1 red onion, finely diced, to garnish

Method

Heat a large pot on a medium heat. Add the mustard seeds and cover with a lid. Once they start to pop, pour in the oil and add the curry leaves, passata and garlic paste. Cook the garlic for 1 minute, until fragrant.

Add the spices and cook for 3–4 minutes until the tomato passata reduces and the spices are well incorporated. Add the tamarind sauce for tangyness, chilli sauce for extra kick and jaggery or sugar for sweetness. Mix everything well, then add the sweetcorn, chickpeas and and potatoes and stir to combine.

Pour in the water, cover with a lid and cook on a low heat for 20 minutes, or until the sauce thickens sightly. Serve in individual bowls, garnished with coriander and red onions.

Mexican-Inspired Savoury Rice

SERVES
3-4

Prep 35 minutes
Cook 40 minutes

A colourful blend of peppers, sweetcorn and black beans in fluffy rice, infused with a blend of zesty flavours and aromatic spices. This mouth-watering savoury rice can be served as a side dish, and is a perfect accompaniment to the Grilled Chipotle Chicken Skewers on page 49.

Ingredients

125g basmati rice

2 tablespoons oil

1 onion, diced

½ red pepper, diced

½ green pepper, diced

200g tinned black beans, drained

150g tinned sweetcorn, drained

2 tablespoons sliced pickled jalapeño chillies

1 teaspoon garlic paste

1 teaspoon ground cumin

1 teaspoon ground coriander

1 teaspoon chilli powder

1 teaspoon hot paprika

1 teaspoon dried oregano

2 tablespoons tomato purée

150g tomato passata

1 teaspoon black pepper

5g fresh coriander, finely chopped, plus extra for garnish

juice of 1 lime, plus extra for garnish

2 vegetable stock cubes

250ml boiling water

salt, to taste

Method

Wash the rice in a sieve under cold running water until the water runs clear.

Heat the oil in a medium pan on a low heat. Add the onion, peppers, black beans, sweetcorn, jalapeños and garlic and sauté for 5 minutes. Add the spices, oregano, tomato purée, tomato passata, black pepper and salt, and cook for another 5 minutes until the tomato passata reduces and the spices are well incorporated.

Add the rice and stir into the vegetables with the fresh coriander and a squeeze of lime juice. Dissolve the vegetable stock cubes in the boiling water and pour into the pan, then partially cover the pan with a lid (do not cover completely or the water may boil over). Cook on a medium heat for 15 minutes, until the water has been absorbed, then give it a stir without disturbing the rice too much. Cover fully with the lid and cook for another 15 minutes on a low heat – the build-up of steam will cook and fluff up the rice.

Garnish with coriander and lime juice, and serve.

FILLING FAMILY

Feasts

✦ • • • • ✦ • • • • ✦

A celebration not just of food, but also of the precious memories that come alive when your nearest and dearest gather around a delicious and stunning spread. These filling and satisfying family meals are perfect for get-togethers and special occasions; the joy of sharing time together creates a warmth and happiness that will stay with you forever.

Lamb Nihari

Prep 20 minutes
Cook 1 hr 30 minutes

SERVES
10

This delicious lamb nihari is my Aunt Khadija's speciality dish. It's a hearty, spicy, meltingly tender stew, with an aromatic, silky smooth and glossy gravy, perfect to scoop up with naan. I promise you, this nihari is ideal for when you have guests.

Ingredients

200ml oil
3 onions, finely sliced
2kg mix of diced lamb shoulder and leg
1 heaped tablespoon ginger paste
1 heaped tablespoon garlic paste
2.5cm piece of fresh root ginger, chopped into small pieces
1 teaspoon ground turmeric
1 teaspoon ground black pepper
1 teaspoon Kashmiri chilli powder
1 teaspoon chilli powder
5 tablespoons nihari masala powder
3 litres water, plus 1 litre hot water
150g wholewheat chapati flour
salt, to taste

WHOLE SPICES
2 bay leaves
2 cinnamon sticks
3 cloves
3 cardamom pods
5–6 black peppercorns
2–3 star anise

TARKA (TO TEMPER THE SPICES)
2 tablespoons oil
1 tablespoon ghee
1 teaspoon cumin seeds

GARNISH
3–4 fresh green chillies, finely sliced
3–4 fresh red chillies, finely sliced
5cm piece fresh root ginger, julienned
10g fresh coriander, finely chopped
2 lemons, cut into wedges
2 limes, cut into wedges

Method

Heat the oil in a large pot on a medium heat, then fry the sliced onions until golden brown, making sure not to burn them, about 20 minutes. Drain on kitchen paper and set aside.

In the same pot, add all the whole spices, the lamb meat, ginger and garlic paste, fresh ginger pieces, turmeric, black pepper and salt. Stir everything together, then cover and cook for 30 minutes on a low heat, making sure to stir occasionally. The water from the meat will evaporate and the oil will float to the top.

Add the chilli powders and nihari masala, cook for 2–3 minutes so the spices are mixed in well, then add 1 litre of cold water. Stir in the fried onions, setting a few aside for the garnish, cover and cook for 20 minutes.

Heat the chapati flour in a frying pan on a low heat for 5 minutes until you can smell the aroma. Transfer the flour to a large bowl, pour in 1 litre of hot water and mix to form a smooth paste. This will act as a thickening agent.

Pour half of the flour mix into the pot of meat, stir in, then pour in the remaining mix and stir again. The nihari will start to thicken. Pour in the remaining 2 litres of cold water, stir, and cover with a lid. Gently simmer on a low heat for 30 minutes until the meat is soft and tender.

For the tarka, heat a medium frying pan on a medium heat, pour in the oil and add the ghee and cumin seeds. Heat for 1 minute until aromatic, then pour over the nihari for an extra layer of flavour.

Serve in bowls and sprinkle with the garnishes: fresh chillies, julienned ginger, the crispy fried onions and fresh coriander. Serve the lemon and lime wedges alongside and squeeze over a little of their juices.

Rawayya, Stuffed Aubergine

Prep 20 minutes
Cook 35 minutes

Rawayya, also known as stuffed aubergine, is a perfect meat-free meal. My grandmother used to make the best stuffed aubergines using small, tender aubergines from our local grocery shop. They were generously stuffed with the mixture of potatoes, peas and tomatoes she so lovingly made, then coated in a blend of Indian spices. I remember sometimes she would also throw in a handful of succulent prawns, which elevated this dish to the next level.

Ingredients

2 onions, finely diced

3 medium potatoes, peeled and cut into small cubes

100g frozen peas

2 vine tomatoes, cut into small pieces

100g tinned chopped tomatoes

1 tablespoon ground cumin

1 tablespoon ground coriander

½ teaspoon ground turmeric

1 teaspoon chilli powder

1 teaspoon cumin seeds

1 teaspoon ginger paste

1 teaspoon garlic paste

1 teaspoon ground black pepper

6 baby aubergines

5 tablespoons oil

5–6 curry leaves

5g fresh coriander, finely chopped, to garnish

salt, to taste

Method

Place the onions, potatoes, peas, fresh tomatoes, tinned tomatoes, ground cumin, ground coriander, ground turmeric, chilli powder, cumin seeds, ginger and garlic pastes, black pepper and salt in a large bowl. Mix everything together and set aside so that the vegetables absorb all the spices.

Rinse and trim the tops of the aubergines, leaving a little stalk. Create a slit in the aubergines lengthways from the bottom up to the stalk area, making sure not to cut all the way to the top. Using your hands or a spoon, stuff the aubergines with the vegetable-spice mixture.

Heat a large, wide-based pan on a low heat, pour in the oil, add the curry leaves and cook for 1 minute until fragrant.

Place the aubergines in the pot with a little water, cover with a lid, and cook for 35 minutes; the build-up of steam will start to cook and soften the aubergine. Make sure to check occasionally that they're not burning or sticking to the pot. Garnish with coriander and serve.

 TIP You can use any variety of aubergine – my favourites are the violet with ivory stripes, known as graffiti aubergines, and Indian aubergines, which are a shiny dark purple, tender and have a sweet taste and aroma.

Steak with Peppercorn Sauce & Creamy Mash

SERVES

4

Prep 20 minutes
Cook 35 minutes

Succulent, beautifully seared steaks draped in a rich, creamy, freshly cracked black peppercorn sauce. These steaks go perfectly with a side of velvety smooth mashed potatoes.

Ingredients

2 tablespoons oil
40g butter
4 fillet steaks, about 1.25cm thickness
crushed black peppercorns, to taste
salt, to taste

PEPPERCORN SAUCE

50g butter
2 cloves garlic, finely chopped
1 tablespoon Worcestershire sauce
3 tablespoons plain flour
250ml double cream
200ml full-fat milk
2 tablespoons black peppercorns, crushed
5g fresh parsley, finely chopped

CREAMY MASH

5 medium potatoes, unpeeled
60g unsalted butter
100ml double cream
120ml full-fat milk
salt, to taste
1 teaspoon chilli flakes, optional

Method

For the creamy mash, bring a large pot of water to the boil and cook the potatoes in their skins for about 25 minutes until tender. Drain and allow to cool slightly, then peel off the skins and place the potatoes in a large bowl. Add the butter, cream, milk, salt and chilli flakes if you want to add some kick to it. Mash well with a potato masher until smooth and creamy.

While the potatoes are cooking, heat a large cast-iron skillet over a medium-high heat. Add the oil. Spread the butter all over the steaks and season with crushed peppercorns and salt. Place the steaks in the hot pan and sear on one side for 3 minutes, then flip and sear the other side for 3 minutes. Transfer to a warm serving plate, cover loosely with foil and keep warm.

Use the same pan to make the peppercorn sauce. Melt the butter on a medium heat, add the garlic, Worcestershire sauce and flour and whisk well to create a smooth paste. Pour in the cream, milk and crushed peppercorns, and continue whisking for 4–5 minutes until the sauce thickens. Season with salt and stir in the chopped parsley. Pour the sauce over the steaks, and serve with the mash alongside.

TIP Any good-quality cut of steak will work, such as ribeye, fillet, porterhouse, T-bone or sirloin.

TIP Sprinkle grated cheese over the cooked mash to make it cheesy.

Coconut Prawn Curry

SERVES

2

Prep 10 minutes
Cook 35 minutes

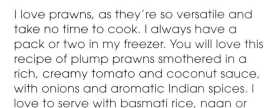

I love prawns, as they're so versatile and take no time to cook. I always have a pack or two in my freezer. You will love this recipe of plump prawns smothered in a rich, creamy tomato and coconut sauce, with onions and aromatic Indian spices. I love to serve with basmati rice, naan or fresh chapati.

Ingredients

2 tablespoons coconut oil or sunflower oil
5 curry leaves
1 teaspoon mustard seeds
2 onions, finely diced
3 garlic cloves, chopped
200g tomato passata or tinned chopped tomatoes
1 teaspoon chilli flakes
1 teaspoon ground cumin
1 teaspoon ground coriander
1 teaspoon Kashmiri chilli powder
250ml coconut milk
300g raw king prawns, peeled and deveined
400ml water
1 fresh red chilli, finely sliced, to garnish
5g fresh coriander, finely chopped, to garnish
salt, to taste

Method

In a medium, wide-based pan on a low heat, add the oil, curry leaves and mustard seeds and fry until fragrant. When the seeds start to pop, add the onions and cook until lightly golden. This can take around 10 minutes.

Add the garlic, tomato passata, chilli flakes, ground cumin, ground coriander and Kashmiri chilli powder, stir, and cook for up to 15 minutes until the tomato has reduced and the oil floats to the top.

Stir in the coconut milk. After a few minutes, the sauce will start to thicken and turn creamy. Add the prawns and water, season with salt, cover, and cook on a medium heat for 8–10 minutes, until the prawns are cooked through.

Garnish with red chillies and chopped fresh coriander.

 To achieve a smooth sauce for a base, I like to use tomato passata, but you can also use tinned tomatoes or fresh tomatoes, blitzed in a food processor.

Lamb Chop Curry

Prep 2–3 hours
Cook 55 minutes

SERVES
5

Cooked in a rich and aromatic curry and infused with traditional store-cupboard Indian spices, these tender and juicy lamb chops are so succulent that they just fall off the bone. This curry is a special dish, perfect for when you have guests over. Serve with basmati rice, naan or fresh chapati.

Ingredients

2 tablespoons Greek yogurt

1 teaspoon ginger paste

1 teaspoon garlic paste

½ teaspoon ground turmeric

20 lamb chops

2 tablespoons sunflower oil

2 bay leaves

2 cinnamon sticks

1 teaspoon cumin seeds

2 onions, finely diced

2 vine tomatoes

2 tablespoons tomato purée

1 teaspoon ground cumin

1 teaspoon ground coriander

1 teaspoon chilli powder

½ teaspoon saffron threads

¼ teaspoon garam masala

5g fresh coriander, finely chopped

salt, to taste

Method

Place the yogurt, ginger paste, garlic paste and ground turmeric in a large bowl. Add the lamb chops, coat in the marinade, and leave to marinate for 2–3 hours in the fridge.

In a large, wide-based pot, add the oil, bay leaves, cinnamon sticks, cumin seeds and onions, and cook until the onions are golden brown, around 20 minutes.

With a knife, score an X in the base of the tomatoes, then submerge them in a bowl of hot water for about 1 minute; the skin will start to loosen and peel away easily. Finely dice the tomatoes and add to the pot along with the tomato purée, ground cumin, ground coriander, chilli powder and salt. Stir, cover, and cook for 5 minutes.

Add the marinated chops to the pot, cover, and cook for 15 minutes on a low-medium heat. The tomatoes will start to reduce.

Infuse the saffron in 2 tablespoons of water and add to the pot. This will enhance the colour and aroma of your curry.

Pour in 600ml water and simmer for 15 minutes until the curry starts to thicken, the chops become cooked through and the oil floats to the top. Sprinkle over the garam masala and chopped fresh coriander.

TIP Marinating the chops for a couple of hours, or even overnight, enhances their flavour, taste and tenderness.

Chicken Handi

Prep 15 minutes
Cook 1 hour 15 minutes

Traditionally, this beautiful dish is made in a handi, which means 'clay pot' in the indian subcontinent – this is where it gets its name from. Cooked over a slow heat, the dish absorbs the aroma of the pot itself. Chicken handi is a flavourful dish of tender boneless chicken cooked in a tomato-onion creamy curry that you can mop up with some bread. Serve with plain rice, chapati or naan.

Ingredients

4 tablespoons oil

2 large onions, puréed

1 teaspoon cumin seeds

1 tablespoon ginger paste

1 tablespoon garlic paste

3 large vine tomatoes, finely chopped

1 teaspoon chilli powder

1 teaspoon ground cumin

1 teaspoon ground coriander

1 teaspoon ground turmeric

1 teaspoon kasuri methi (dried fenugreek leaves)

600g boneless chicken breasts or thighs, cut into bite-sized pieces

400ml water

200ml Greek yogurt

½ teaspoon garam masala, to garnish

5g fresh coriander, finely chopped, to garnish

3–4 fresh green chillies, halved, to garnish

salt, to taste

Method

Heat the oil in a large wok or stainless-steel karahi on a medium heat, then add the onions and cumin seeds. Stir, and fry the onions until golden brown, about 20 minutes. Add the ginger and garlic paste and cook for 1 minute, then add the tomatoes, chilli powder, ground cumin, ground coriander, ground turmeric and kasuri methi, stir to combine, and cook for 15 minutes until the tomatoes are reduced and the oil separates.

Add the chicken pieces and combine well with the rest of the ingredients. Cover and cook for 20 minutes on a low heat, or until no moisture is left.

Pour in the water and yogurt. Season with salt, cover, and cook on a low heat for another 20 minutes, or until the chicken is tender and cooked through. Stir occasionally, adding more water if you want a saucier consistency. The aroma around your kitchen will be amazing!

Transfer to a copper-bottomed serving handi, if you have one, or a serving dish and garnish with a sprinkling of garam masala, chopped coriander and fresh green chillies.

 A good sign that a curry is cooking well is when the masala turns shiny and the oil separates and floats to the top.

Fish Biryani

Prep 30 minutes
Marinate 1 hour
Cook 45 minutes

The ultimate family meal, fish biryani is one of my favourite rice dishes. Flavourful chunks of fish marinated in traditional Indian spices, carefully layered with aromatic basmati rice… as you lift the lid of the biryani pot, the mouth-watering aroma spreads throughout the kitchen. I enjoyed visiting the fishmonger's with my grandmother; now I love taking my children to look at all the different and colourful varieties of freshly caught fish.

Ingredients

5 tablespoons oil, plus extra for deep-frying

3 large onions, finely sliced

2 tablespoons garlic paste

2 tablespoons green chilli paste

1 tablespoon ground cumin

1 tablespoon ground coriander

2 teaspoons chilli powder

1 teaspoon ground turmeric

10g fresh coriander, finely chopped, plus extra to finish

10g fresh mint, finely chopped, plus extra to finish

1 teaspoon black pepper, crushed

300g tinned chopped tomatoes, puréed

10 cod loins or fillets, cut in half

2 tablespoons ghee

½ red pepper, cut into 2.5cm chunks

½ green pepper, cut into 2.5cm chunks

4 tablespoons finely sliced spring onions

juice of 1 lemon, plus lemon wedges to serve

1 teaspoon saffron threads

2 tablespoons milk

salt, to taste

RICE

600g basmati rice

1.5 litres water

2 tablespoons oil

1 tablespoon salt

2 cinnamon sticks

2 bay leaves

salt, to taste

Method

Heat the oil for deep-frying in a large pot on a medium-high heat until it reaches 180°C. Fry the sliced onions until golden brown, making sure not to burn them, about 15 minutes. Drain on kitchen paper and leave to cool a little.

Reserve a few fried onions for garnish, then put the remainder in a large bowl with the garlic paste, chilli paste, ground cumin, ground coriander, chilli powder, ground turmeric, fresh coriander, fresh mint and black pepper. Blitz the tomatoes in a food processor and add to the bowl. Mix everything together to combine.

Rinse and pat dry the cod loins, then place in the bowl with the marinade, coat the loins all over and leave to marinate in the fridge for 1 hour.

To prepare the rice, wash in a sieve under cold running water until the water runs clear, then soak in a bowl of cold water for 30 minutes. This will reduce the cooking time and help the rice to cook evenly.

Pour the water into a large saucepan, bring to the boil and add the oil, salt, cinnamon sticks and bay leaves. Add the rice and cook, uncovered, for 8–10 minutes until it is 80–85 per cent cooked. It needs to be cooked on the outside, but the inside should be a little firm as the rice will cook further when you cook the biryani. Drain in a colander, then rinse under cold running water to stop it from cooking further. Drain well, then spread the rice on a large plate and leave to cool completely, so the grains are separate and the rice does not become mushy.

Grease the bottom of a large wide-based pot with ghee and arrange half the rice in an even layer at the bottom. Top with the marinated fish, scatter over the red and green pepper chunks and spring onions and squeeze over some lemon juice. Then add the remaining rice on top in an even layer.

Place the saffron threads in a small frying pan on a very low heat and warm through for no longer than 1 minutes, taking care as the strands burn easily. When slightly crisp, crush with the back of a spoon and add to the milk. Drizzle over the saffron-infused milk to add aroma and colour to the rice, then scatter over the remaining fried onions and a sprinkling of fresh coriander and mint.

Poke some holes in the rice to allow steam to escape and drizzle a little water into the holes. Dot ghee over the top of the rice to add extra flavour. Cover the pot with a tight-fitting lid, so the steam doesn't escape the pot, and cook on low heat for 20 minutes. With the build-up of steam, the fish will cook through, the rice will fluff up and the biryani will be ready. Serve on a large platter with some lemon wedges.

Recipe photo overleaf.

 TIP You can also add fried potatoes to the biryani. Peel some baby potatoes, cut in half and deep-fry until golden. Place on top of the biryani when serving.

Lamb Jalfrezi

Prep 20 minutes
Cook 1 hour 15 minutes

The aroma of this lamb jalfrezi will make your mouth water – it's so good, I know your plate will be wiped clean. The flavour is phenomenal, with succulent pieces of lamb, golden-brown onions, tangy tomatoes, warming spices, a subtle taste of fenugreek and heat from the chillies. Serve with basmati rice or naan and salad.

Ingredients

2 tablespoons sunflower oil

½ teaspoon cumin seeds

½ teaspoon nigella seeds

2 onions, finely sliced

800g boneless lamb, cut into 2.5cm chunks

1 teaspoon garlic paste

1 teaspoon ginger paste

250g tinned chopped tomatoes

1 teaspoon chilli powder

1 teaspoon ground cumin

1 teaspoon ground coriander

1 teaspoon Kashmiri chilli powder

½ teaspoon ground turmeric

½ teaspoon dried fenugreek

2 tablespoons tomato purée

¼ teaspoon garam masala

½ red pepper, cut into 2.5cm chunks

½ green pepper, cut into 2.5cm chunks

1 red onion, cut into 2.5cm chunks

300ml water

5g fresh coriander, finely chopped

salt, to taste

Method

In a large, wide-based pan on a medium heat, add the oil, cumin seeds, nigella seeds and onions, and fry until the onions are golden brown, about 15 minutes.

Add the lamb, garlic paste and ginger paste, stir to combine, then reduce the heat to low and cook, covered, for 30–40 minutes, stirring occasionally, until the lamb is tender.

Blitz the tinned tomatoes in a food processor, then add to the pan with the chilli powder, ground cumin, ground coriander, Kashmiri chilli powder, ground turmeric and dried fenugreek. Stir 4 tablespoons of water into the tomato purée and add to the pan. Continue to cook on a low heat until the tomatoes reduce and the oil floats to the top. This can take around 15 minutes.

Add the garam masala, peppers, red onion and water and simmer for 10 minutes until the consistency is gravy-like. Garnish with chopped fresh coriander.

 If you have a pressure cooker, it will cut the cooking time of this dish in half.

Beef Kheema Biryani

Prep 30 minutes
Cook 1 hour 15 minutes

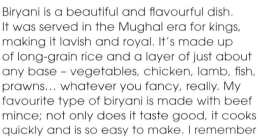

Biryani is a beautiful and flavourful dish. It was served in the Mughal era for kings, making it lavish and royal. It's made up of long-grain rice and a layer of just about any base – vegetables, chicken, lamb, fish, prawns… whatever you fancy, really. My favourite type of biryani is made with beef mince; not only does it taste good, it cooks quickly and is so easy to make. I remember my mum layering up the biryani, making sure to leave some masala in the pot for me and my brother to mop up with chapati or bread. The typical accompaniment in our home was sweet lassi, poppodoms and pickles.

Ingredients

1 teaspoon saffron threads

2 tablespoons milk

2 tablespoons ghee

10g fresh coriander leaves, finely chopped, plus extra to garnish

2–3 japalpeño chillies, halved

80ml water

1 lemon, cut into wedges, to garnish

KHEEMA MASALA

5 tablespoons sunflower oil, plus extra for deep-frying

5 onions, finely sliced

1kg beef mince

1 tablespoon ginger paste

1 tablespoon garlic paste

6 tablespoons tinned chopped tomatoes

50g frozen peas

1 tablespoon ground cumin

1 tablespoon ground coriander

1 tablespoon chilli powder

1 teaspoon ground black pepper

½ teaspoon garam masala

salt, to taste

WHOLE SPICES

2 star anise

1 teaspoon cumin seeds

2 cinnamon sticks

2 bay leaves

5 black peppercorns

5 cardamom pods

5 cloves

RICE

700g basmati rice

2½ litres water

3 tablespoons sunflower oil

2 bay leaves

2 cinnamon sticks

1 tablespoon salt

Method

To prepare the kheema masala, heat the oil for deep-frying in a large pan on a medium-high heat until it reaches 180°C. Deep-fry the sliced onions for up to 20 minutes until golden brown, making sure they don't burn, then drain on kitchen paper and set aside.

To prepare the rice, wash the rice in a sieve under cold running water until the water runs clear, then soak in a bowl of cold water for 30 minutes. This will reduce the cooking time and help the rice to cook evenly.

Pour the water for the rice into a large pot. Bring to the boil, then add the oil, bay leaves, cinnamon sticks and salt. Add the rice and cook, uncovered, for 8–10 minutes until it is three-quarters cooked. It needs to be cooked on the outside but the inside should be a little firm as the rice will cook further with the biryani. Drain, then rinse under cold running water to stop it from cooking further. Drain well, then spread the rice on a large plate and leave to cool completely, so the grains are separated and the rice does not go mushy.

For the kheema masala, heat the 5 tablespoons of oil in a large saucepan on a low heat, add the whole spices and allow them to gently infuse in the oil for 30 seconds. Add the beef mince and break up any lumps with a wooden spoon. Add the ginger and garlic pastes, stir, then cover and cook for 30 minutes until the water released from the mince has evaporated.

Blitz the tomatoes in a food processor and add to the pan with half the fried onions, setting the rest aside for garnish. Add the frozen peas, ground cumin, ground coriander, chilli powder, black pepper and salt. Mix everything together and cook for 15 minutes on a low-medium heat until the masala starts to thicken. Sprinkle over the garam masala to add some warmth to the masala.

Place the saffron threads in a small frying pan on a very low heat and warm through for 40 seconds, taking care as the strands burn easily. When slightly crisp, crush with the back of a spoon, add to the milk and set aside.

Grease the bottom of a large, wide-based pan with a little of the ghee and arrange half the rice in an even layer at the bottom. Top with the mince mixture and sprinkle with a few of the remaining fried onions, half of the chopped coriander and the halved jalapeño chillies. Spread the remaining rice over the top in an even layer. Drizzle over the saffron-infused milk to add aroma and colour to the rice, then finally scatter over the remaining fried onions and chopped coriander.

Poke some holes in the rice to allow steam to escape and drizzle the water into the holes. Dot the remaining ghee over the top of the rice to add extra flavour. Cover the pot with a tight-fitting lid so the steam doesn't escape and cook on a low heat for 20 minutes. With the build-up of steam, the rice will finish cooking and fluff up and the biryani will be ready. Serve on a large platter, garnished with chopped fresh coriander and lemon wedges.

 I like to add fried potatoes to my biryani. Just peel and cut the potato into quarters, deep-fry until golden, then place on top of the biryani and serve. You could also add some boiled eggs!

Cauliflower, Potato & Pea Curry

SERVES
4–5

Prep 20 minutes
Cook 30 minutes

This hearty and heart-warming vegetarian curry comes together in no time, perfect for when you feel like cooking up a meat-free feast for the family. The nutty flavour of the cauliflower, the tender sweetness of the peas and the satisfying taste of the potatoes are combined with a rich aromatic tomato-based gravy made with a blend of Indian spices. Enjoy this curry with chapatis, naan or basmati rice.

Ingredients

400g cauliflower, cut into florets
2 medium potatoes, peeled and cut into chunks
4 tablespoons oil
1 teaspoon cumin seeds
1 tablespoon curry leaves
2 onions, finely diced
1 teaspoon garlic paste
1 teaspoon chilli powder
½ teaspoon ground turmeric
1 teaspoon ground cumin
1 teaspoon ground coriander
300g tomato passata
500ml water
300g frozen or fresh peas
½ red pepper, cut into small chunks
5g fresh coriander, finely chopped, to garnish
salt, to taste

Method

In a large pan of boiling water, par-cook the cauliflower and potatoes for about 5 minutes, making sure you don't overcook them or they will go mushy. Drain in a colander.

Heat a large pan on a medium heat, then add the oil, cumin seeds, curry leaves and onions and fry until golden brown, about 20 minutes.

Add the garlic paste, chilli powder, ground turmeric, ground cumin, ground coriander and salt. Mix everything together and cook for 2–3 minutes, so the spices blend nicely.

Add the tomato passata and cook on a medium-high heat until the passata has reduced and thickened and the oil separates and floats to the top.

After the passata has reduced and thickened, mix in the cauliflower and potatoes, until coated well in the tomato masala.

Pour in the water and stir in the peas and red pepper, then cover and cook on a low heat for 20 minutes, stirring occasionally. The curry will thicken slightly. Garnish with chopped coriander and serve.

Zarda, Sweet Rice

SERVES

6-7

Prep 20 minutes
Cook 1 hour

Zarda is a sweet rice dish popular in most Indian homes. It's so vibrant and rich, and is often served at weddings, on special occasions, and when you have guests over for Eid celebrations. On Eid day, my mum would prepare a big pot of zarda and the kitchen would be filled with the sweet aroma of nuts, dried fruits and spices.

Ingredients

3 tablespoons ghee or clarified butter

2 tablespoons sultanas

2 tablespoons almonds, halved

2 tablespoons cashews

2 tablespoons pistachios, chopped or whole, as preferred

2 cinnamon sticks

5 cardamom pods

3 tablespoons tinned pineapple chunks

1 teaspoon cardamom powder

2 tablespoons glace cherries, halved

RICE

2.5 litres water

400g rice

1 teaspoon lemon juice

½ teaspoon ground turmeric

SUGAR SYRUP

500ml water

300g granulated sugar

½ teaspoon saffron threads

½ teaspoon cardamom powder

Method

To make the rice, boil the water, lemon juice and turmeric in a large pot on a medium-high heat. Wash the rice and add to the pot. Cook the rice until it's 95 per cent done, about 12–15 minutes, then drain in a colander and rinse under cold water to stop it from cooking further. Set aside.

For the sugar syrup, heat the water, sugar, saffron threads and cardamom powder in a saucepan on low-medium heat for 40 minutes, stirring occasionally. The syrup will simmer gently and start to reduce, then turn slightly sticky and thicken – that's when you know it's done. Set aside to cool.

In a large pot on a low heat, cook the ghee, sultanas, almonds, cashews, pistachios, cinnamon sticks and cardamom pods for 2–3 minutes. The sultanas will start to plump up and you should be able to smell the aroma.

Add the rice, pineapple chunks and cardamom powder to the pot and pour over the syrup. Stir gently, making sure not to break the rice. Cover with a lid and cook on a low heat until the syrup has reduced.

Transfer to a serving platter and decorate with the glace cherries on top.

Gajar Halwa, Carrot Halwa

SERVES
6–7

Prep 20 minutes
Cook 50 minutes

Gajar halwa, also known as carrot halwa, is a beloved Indian sweet dessert. Served on special occasions, and at festivals and family gatherings, it looks beautiful on any dinner table. The key ingredient of gajar halwa is of course the humble carrot, which is grated and cooked in milk, bringing out the natural sweetness of the carrots and really enhancing the flavour. You can serve this decadent dessert cold or warm, but I prefer the latter, with a scoop of creamy vanilla ice cream, which really complements the halwa. You will enjoy every bite!

Ingredients

1kg carrots, peeled and grated
400ml milk
125g ghee or clarified butter
125g desiccated coconut
125g condensed milk
125g granulated sugar
125g milk powder
5–6 almonds, chopped, plus extra to garnish
5–6 cashews, whole, plus extra to garnish
5–6 pistachios, chopped, plus extra to garnish
1/2 teaspoon ground cardamom
1 teaspoon saffron threads, to garnish

Method

Heat a large pot on a medium heat. Add the grated carrots, pour over the milk, reduce the heat to low and simmer for 45 minutes until all the liquid has evaporated. Make sure to stir occasionally so the carrots don't burn.

Add the ghee and mix until melted, then stir in the coconut and condensed milk. The mixture will look fudgy. Sprinkle in the sugar and continue to cook until it has dissolved, 5–6 minutes.

Reduce to a low heat and add the milk powder and mix for 3–4 minutes until incorporated nicely. Sprinkle over the almonds, cashews, pistachios and ground cardamom to add fragrance, and mix everything together.

Serve in individual dessert cups or bowls, garnished with more nuts and a few strands of saffron.

 Roast the almonds and cashews for added crunch.

 For a rich, creamy taste, always use full-fat milk.

15-Minute

SNACKS

✦ ·◦·⚬·◦· ✦ ·◦·⚬·◦· ✦

Welcome to the delightful world of 15-minute snacks! We have all experienced those days when time isn't on our side, or when we're simply craving a quick bite. You'll find a collection of speedy, effortless dishes here that are big on flavour but short on time, and just perfect for such moments.

Desi Omelette

Prep 5 minutes
Cook 5–6 minutes

SERVES
4-5

- - - - - - - + - - - - + - - - - + - - - - + - - - -

Desi omelette is a traditional Indian version of the classic omelette. Its beauty lies in its versatility – you can get creative and adjust it to your taste preference, adding different spices, herbs and vegetables. It's very popular at breakfast time, but is so quick and easy to make that you can have it any time of the day. Serve with Masala Beans (see page 114) and chapati.

Ingredients

6 eggs
1 teaspoon chilli powder
½ teaspoon ground turmeric
1 teaspoon ground cumin
1 teaspoon ground black pepper
1 red onion, finely diced
1/2 red pepper, cut into small cubes
2 garlic cloves, crushed
2 spring onions, finely chopped
5g fresh coriander, finely chopped
1 green chilli, finely chopped (optional, for an extra kick!)
2 tablespoons oil
salt, to taste

Method

Crack the eggs into a bowl and add the chilli powder, ground turmeric, ground cumin, black pepper, onion, red pepper, garlic, spring onions, coriander, fresh chilli, if using, and salt to taste. Whisk it all up with a fork.

Heat the oil in a medium frying pan on a medium heat. Pour the egg mixture into the heated pan and swirl the pan to spread the eggs evenly. You can cook the egg mixture in batches if needed. Cover the pan with a lid and cook for 3–4 minutes until the bottom side is set and browned lightly.

Using a flat spatula, flip the omelette and cook the other side uncovered for 1–2 minutes.

 TIP To make your omelette cheesy, sprinkle grated cheese over the top once flipped, then cover, and it will melt nicely.

Masala Beans

Prep 15 minutes
Cook 15 minutes

SERVES
4

Baked beans with an Indian twist, and one of my childhood favourites. I remember my mum making this dish with fresh chapatis and fried eggs, and I will often make it with the kids for a weekend breakfast. I guarantee these beans will jazz up any meal or snack time. Garnish with fresh coriander and serve with Masala Omelette (see page 112) and chapati.

Ingredients

2 tablespoons oil

1 teaspoon cumin seeds

1 onion, finely diced

1 tablespoon tomato purée

2 garlic cloves, crushed

1 teaspoon chilli powder

½ teaspoon ground turmeric

1 teaspoon ground coriander

1 teaspoon ground cumin

2 x 400g tins of baked beans

fresh coriander leaves, to garnish

salt, to taste

Method

Heat the oil in a small pan over a medium heat. Add the cumin seeds and onion and fry for 12 minutes or until soft and lightly golden.

Add the tomato purée, garlic, chilli powder, ground turmeric, ground coriander, ground cumin and salt. Cook the spices for 1 minute, then add the baked beans and cook on a low heat for 2–3 minutes.

Chickpea Chaat

Prep 15 minutes

SERVES
4-5

Chickpea chaat is a spicy, tangy street food. Simple, refreshing and bursting with flavour in every spoonful, the yogurt is creamy and cooling. If you want to spice things up, you can add a sliced fresh green chilli! Serve with Spicy Vegetable Samosas (page 36).

Ingredients

2 x 400g tins of chickpeas, drained
2 medium tomatoes, diced
1 red onion, diced
2 tablespoons fresh mint leaves, finely chopped
2 tablespoons fresh coriander leaves, plus extra to garnish
300g Greek yogurt

½ teaspoon chilli flakes
1 teaspoon chaat masala, plus extra for sprinkling
2 tablespoons tamarind sauce
seeds of 1 pomegranate, to garnish
salt, to taste

Method

Place the chickpeas, tomatoes, red onion, mint, coriander, yogurt, chilli flakes and chaat masala in a large bowl. Add salt to taste and mix together. Drizzle over the tamarind sauce.

Garnish with fresh coriander, pomegranate seeds and a sprinkling of chaat masala.

Sweetcorn Chaat

Prep 5 minutes
Cook 2 minutes

SERVES
2

A popular Indian street food, made with sweetcorn, red and green peppers and a handful of spices.

Ingredients

200g tinned sweetcorn kernels, drained
½ tsp garlic granules
½ tsp hot paprika
½ tsp chilli powder
½ tsp ground black pepper
½ tsp dried parsley
½ red pepper, cut into small chunks
½ green pepper, cut into small chunks
juice of ½ lemon

Method

Place a small saucepan on a low heat. Add the sweetcorn, garlic granules, paprika, chilli powder, pepper, parsley, red and green pepper chunks and stir to combine. Heat gently for 2 minutes.

Pour over the lemon juice and serve immediately.

 TIP After squeezing the lemon, if you want to make it creamy, add 2 tablespoons of mayonnaise, or make it cheesy by sprinkling over a handful of grated cheese of your choice.

Aloo Pakora,
Spicy Potato Fritters

MAKES
30

Prep 15 minutes
Cook 3 minutes

Aloo pakora, also known as potato fritters, is a popular golden and crunchy Indian snack. The chickpea batter is spiced with ground cumin, which adds a warm and earthy flavour; carom (ajwain) seeds, which are slightly pungent and add a pleasant aroma to the pakora; ground fenugreek, which enhances the taste; and chilli powder and chilli flakes for a spicy kick. Crispy on the outside and soft and tender on the inside, these are incredibly delicious and will disappear from the platter as soon as they are served.

Ingredients

125g chickpea flour
25g rice flour
1 teaspoon chilli powder
1 teaspoon chilli flakes
1 teaspoon carom seeds (ajwain), lightly crushed
1 teaspoon ground cumin
½ teaspoon ground turmeric
1 teaspoon ground fenugreek
5g fresh coriander, finely chopped
60ml water
oil, for deep-frying
2 large potatoes, peeled and cut into 0.5cm slices
salt, to taste

Method

Place the flours, chilli powder, chilli flakes, carom seeds, ground cumin, ground turmeric, ground fenugreek, fresh coriander and salt in a large bowl.

Pour in enough of the water to create a thick, paste-like consistency, giving everything a mix. If the batter is too thick, add a little more water.

Heat the oil for deep-frying in a large saucepan on a medium heat until it reaches 180°C. Drop a little of the batter into the oil – if it sizzles, the oil is ready.

Dip each potato slice into the batter, making sure to coat them properly. Carefully transfer to the hot oil, making sure not to overcrowd the pan. You may need to do this in batches.

Fry for 2–3 minutes, flipping the potato slices occasionally, until both sides are golden.

Remove the fritters with a slotted spoon and drain off any excess oil in a colander. Serve with your favourite dip.

 Feel free to experiment using any vegetable you have to hand. Aubergine is a good option, as the inside is soft, which contrasts well with the crispy batter on the outside.

Pitta Bread Pizza

Prep 5 minutes
Cook 10 minutes

SERVES
1

If you or your children are craving a pizza, this colourful pitta bread version is perfect. It's easy, and ever so flavoursome. Pitta bread makes a great base for pizza. Even my husband Adam remembers making these when he got home from school!

Ingredients

1 heaped tablespoon tomato purée
1 pitta bread, wholemeal or white
2 tablespoons grated mozzarella cheese
2 tablespoons tinned sweetcorn kernels, drained
½ red pepper, cut into small chunks
½ green pepper, cut into small chunks
2 black olives, sliced
½ teaspoon ground black pepper
½ teaspoon dried oregano
salt, to taste

Method

Preheat your oven to 180°C (gas mark 4).

Spread the tomato purée over the pitta bread. Sprinkle over the mozzarella cheese, sweetcorn, red and green peppers, black olives, pepper and oregano.

Bake for 10 minutes, or until the cheese has melted and turned golden brown.

 Level up your pitta pizza by adding leftover roast chicken or tinned tuna on top. Or for a spicy kick, add some jalapeños or chilli flakes – or both!

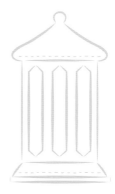

Mixed Beans Cheesy Quesadilla

SERVES
2

Prep 10 minutes
Cook 15 minutes

This is the perfect snack when you want something quick and filling. The quesadillas are stuffed with tasty spiced mixed beans and melted cheese.

Ingredients

1 tablespoon olive oil

1 onion, finely diced

1 teaspoon garlic paste

400g tin mixed beans, drained

½ red pepper, cut into small chunks

1 tablespoon chipotle chilli paste

½ teaspoon ground black pepper

2 tortilla wraps

3g fresh coriander, finely chopped

100g grated cheese, cheddar or mozzarella

juice of 1 lime

tomato salsa (I use pre-prepared from a jar)

salt, to taste

Method

Heat the oil in a medium pan over a medium heat and fry the onions for about 5 minutes until soft. Add the garlic paste, mixed beans, red pepper, chipotle chilli paste and black pepper and season with salt. Stir everything together, cover, and heat through for 3–4 minutes.

Sprinkle over the fresh coriander, then gently mash the mixture with a spoon, leaving the mixture quite rough.

Heat a frying pan large enough to hold a tortilla. Place one tortilla in the pan, spread the bean mixture evenly over it, sprinkle with the cheese, squeeze some lime juice inside, and top with the second tortilla. After 3–4 minutes the tortilla on the bottom will start to brown and slightly toast.

Carefully flip the tortilla to toast the other side until it also starts to brown. Cut into quarters and enjoy with salsa..

Tuna Lettuce Cups

Prep 15 minutes

MAKES
6

Tuna lettuce cups are a great quick lunch option, perfect for those busy days when time is not on your side.

Ingredients

6 Little Gem or Romaine lettuce leaves
2 x 145g tins of tuna, drained
5 tablespoons mayonnaise
200g tin of sweetcorn, drained
1 small red onion, diced
½ red pepper, diced
1 teaspoon chilli flakes
1 teaspoon ground black pepper
4 tablespoons sweet chilli sauce
8 cherry tomatoes, halved
3g fresh parsley, chopped
juice of 1 lime
salt, to taste

Method

Gently rinse the lettuce leaves and pat them dry.

Place the tuna in a bowl with the mayonnaise, sweetcorn kernels, red onion, red pepper, chilli flakes, black pepper and sweet chilli sauce. Mix until thoroughly combined.

Place the lettuce leaves on a platter. Divide the tuna salad evenly between them and top with the cherry tomatoes, fresh parsley and a squeeze of lime.

 Try this with leftover chicken instead of the tuna – you'll love it!

Chilli & Garlic Prawns

SERVES
3

Prep 10 minutes
Cook 5 minutes

These prawns are perfect when you're feeling peckish and want a quick bite to eat. I often make this dish for my family, when it's been a busy day and I need to rustle up something simple but delicious. The delightful combination of juicy prawns, pungent garlic and fiery chillies creates a fusion of flavours and will tempt your taste buds.

Ingredients

30g unsalted butter

1 tablespoon olive oil

2 garlic cloves, finely chopped

1 fresh red chilli, finely sliced

170g raw king prawns, cleaned and deveined

½ teaspoon chilli powder

½ teaspoon chilli flakes

1 tablespoon sriracha sauce

1 teaspoon light soy sauce

3g fresh parsley, chopped, to garnish

1 spring onion, finely sliced, to garnish

1 lemon, cut into wedges, to garnish

salt, to taste

Method

Melt the butter and oil in a large wok on a low heat.

Add the garlic and fresh chilli, stir and cook for 1 minute or until fragrant.

Add the prawns, chilli powder, chilli flakes, sriracha sauce and soy sauce. Cook, stirring occasionally, for 7–8 minutes, until the water released from the prawns has evaporated and the oil comes through to the top.

Garnish with chopped parsley, spring onion and lemon wedges, and eat on its own, with salad or on a slice of toast.

Bake it

EASY

✦ · · ◦ · · ✦ · · ✦ · · ◦ · · ✦

There is something so comforting and magical about homemade treats. I have always loved to bake, and especially the enticing aroma that fills the kitchen. Here you will find a collection of beautiful, buttery biscuits and fluffy, soft, cloud-like cakes. So put on your apron and let this baking journey take you to a place where time slows down and each moment becomes a cherished memory.

Orange & Almond Loaf

MAKES
10

Prep 45 minutes
Cook 1 hour 15 minutes

This loaf is so moist and soft, with a beautifully crumbly texture. Packed with fresh orange flavour in each bite, it is topped with a light orange glaze and finished beautifully with dried orange slices. Your family is in for a treat!

Ingredients

150g butter, at room temperature, plus extra for greasing
130g light brown sugar
2 eggs
50g ground almonds
2 tablespoons grated orange zest
2 tablespoons fresh orange juice
150g self-raising flour
½ teaspoon baking powder
edible fresh flowers, to garnish (optional)

ORANGE & HONEY SYRUP
1 tablespoon honey
2 tablespoons fresh orange juice

ORANGE SLICES
1 orange, thinly sliced
2 tablespoons granulated sugar

ICING
200g icing sugar
3 tablespoons fresh orange juice

TIP When preparing the orange slices, the thinner the orange is sliced, the quicker the slices will dry out in the oven.

Method

Preheat the oven to 160°C (gas mark 3). Grease and line a loaf tin approximately 21.5 x 11cm with baking paper.

Cream the butter and brown sugar together until light and fluffy using an electric hand whisk or wooden spoon. Gradually add the eggs and whisk until well combined. Stir in the ground almonds and orange zest, then pour in the fresh orange juice and give everything a good mix. Gently fold in the flour and baking powder, but do not over mix at this stage.

Pour the mixture into the loaf tin and bake for 40 minutes, until the cake is golden on top and a skewer inserted into the centre comes out clean. Set aside in the tin while you make the syrup. Leave the oven on and increase the heat to 180°C (gas mark 4).

For the syrup, combine the honey and orange juice in a bowl. Poke the loaf all over using a skewer, then brush the top of your loaf with the syrup. The syrup will keep the loaf moist and soft.

To make the orange slices, line a baking tray with baking paper. Cut the slices in half, coat them in the sugar, then arrange on the lined baking tray with a little space between each one. Bake in the oven for 30 minutes, until the edges are golden and the slices have dried out. Set aside to cool.

To make the icing, sift the icing sugar into a bowl. Pour in the orange juice and whisk until smooth and glossy. Pour the icing over the loaf and decorate with the dried oranges.

Zesty Lemon Drizzle Cake

SERVES
16

Prep 20 minutes
Cook 25 minutes

One of my favourite cakes, this one is bursting with zesty lemon flavour, and is so moist and light that it just melts in your mouth. I bake this for Eid, to share with my neighbours on a platter among other sweet treats, but you can make it any time you're craving this beautiful fresh, zingy cake.

Ingredients

170g margarine, at room temperature
150g caster sugar
3 eggs
2 tablespoons milk
grated zest and juice of 1 lemon
200g self-raising flour
½ teaspoon baking powder

DRIZZLE TOPPING
180g granulated sugar
grated zest and juice of 2 lemons
1 teaspoon dried cornflower petals (optional)

Method

Preheat the oven to 160°C (gas mark 3). Line a 20 x 20cm square cake tin with baking paper.

Cream the margarine and sugar together until light and fluffy using an electric hand whisk or wooden spoon. Add the eggs one at a time, mixing well after each addition. Add the milk, lemon zest and juice and mix well. Gently fold in the flour and baking powder, but do not over mix at this stage.

Pour the mixture into the prepared tin, spread evenly and smooth the top with a spatula. Bake for 25 minutes, or until the cake is golden on top and a skewer inserted into the centre comes out clean. Set aside in the tin while you make the drizzle topping.

In a medium bowl, combine the granulated sugar and lemon juice until the sugar dissolves.

While the cake is still warm, poke several holes all over the top and pour the lemon drizzle over, making sure it seeps into the holes. Decorate with the lemon zest and sprinkle over dried cornflower petals, if desired, to pretty it up. Leave to cool; the topping will become white and crunchy. Cut into equal squares and serve.

Easy Chocolate Traybake

SERVES
20

Prep 15 minutes
Cooks 50 minutes

The perfect chocolate cake, with decadent fudgy chocolate icing. This traybake is absolutely divine and utterly scrumptious. My children love all things chocolate, so they love making this cake, and I'm sure you will too!

Ingredients

100ml sunflower oil
100ml milk
2 eggs, beaten
1 teaspoon vanilla essence
150g plain flour
50g cocoa powder
250g caster sugar
1 teaspoon baking powder
1 teaspoon bicarbonate of soda
100ml hot water
colourful sprinkles, to decorate

ICING
160ml double cream
1 teaspoon vanilla essence
50g butter
180g milk chocolate
50g icing sugar

Method

Preheat the oven to 160°C (gas mark 3). Grease and line a 30 x 22cm cake tin with baking paper.

Combine the oil, milk, eggs and vanilla essence in a mixing bowl.

Into another bowl, sift the flour, cocoa powder, sugar, baking powder and bicarbonate of soda.

Add the dry ingredients to the bowl with the wet mixture and beat until smooth. Pour in the hot water and mix gently until everything is incorporated nicely, making sure not to over mix.

Pour the mixture into the tin and bake for 45–50 minutes, until a skewer inserted into the centre comes out clean. Set aside to cool in the tin for 20 minutes, then remove from the tin and leave to cool on a wire cooling rack.

For the icing, place the cream, vanilla essence, butter and milk chocolate into a medium saucepan. Sift the icing sugar into the pan and stir gently over a low-medium heat for 10–12 minutes, until the chocolate has melted and the icing is smooth.

Leave the icing to cool and thicken, about 1 hour. Spread the icing over the traybake and decorate with colourful sprinkles. Stored in an airtight container, the traybake will keep for up to 5 days.

Date & Nut Dainties

Prep 45 minutes
Cook 15 minutes

MAKES
20

I love sharing sweet treats with friends and family, and these dainties are always on my baking list for Eid. They're packed with nuts, dates and coconut, making them so scrumptious and irresistible.

Ingredients

125g unsalted butter
40g caster sugar
1 egg
1 teaspoon vanilla essence
80g dates, chopped
60g pecans, chopped
100g desiccated coconut, plus extra for rolling
60g plain flour
10 glace cherries, quartered, for decoration

Method

Line a baking tray with parchment paper and preheat the oven to 160°C.

Cream the butter and sugar together until light and fluffy using an electric hand whisk or wooden spoon. Add the egg and vanilla essence and whisk again for 1 minute until the egg is incorporated.

Stir in the dates, pecans, desiccated coconut and flour, then use your hands to mix everything together to form a dough. The dough will be slightly sticky, but that's fine.

Roll the dough into small balls, weighing approximately 20g each, so they are all equal.

Roll the balls in desiccated coconut and place the tray, leaving space in between as they will expand a little. Place a cherry quarter on each one for decoration.

Bake for 15 minutes, until lightly golden. Stored in an airtight container, these will keep for up to a week.

Summer Berry Pavlova

SERVES
8

Prep 25 minutes
Cook 1 hr

How pretty is this perfect, simple summer dessert? Light and airy, crunchy on the outside, marshmallowy on the inside, with a dreamy, creamy topping – it is so indulgent and a spectacular centrepiece for any occasion. You'll absolutely fall in love with how easy and delicious it is!

Ingredients

4 egg whites
¼ teaspoon cream of tartar or white wine vinegar
200g granulated sugar
100g strawberries
100g raspberries
100g blueberries
100g blackberries

TOPPING
150g mascarpone
300ml double cream
4 tablespoons icing sugar, to sweeten

 Dust with icing sugar and decorate with edible fresh flowers to add a lovely finishing touch to your dessert.

Method

Preheat the oven to 120°C (gas mark ½) and line a baking tray with baking paper.

Add the egg whites to the bowl of a stand mixer fitted with a balloon whisk attachment and beat until soft peaks form. With the mixer still running, very slowly add the cream of tartar (or vinegar) and sugar, and whisk on high until glossy and stiff peaks form. This could take up to 5 minutes.

Spoon the meringue onto the baking tray and spread into a circle approximately 20–25cm in diameter and 5cm thick. Bake for 1 hour or until crisp on the outside and softer on the inside. Leave the meringue to cool completely.

To make the topping, use an electric hand whisk to whip the mascarpone, cream and sugar together until soft peaks form.

Assemble the pavlova just before serving. Pile the mascarpone cream in the centre of the meringue, then spread to the edge, leaving around 2.5cm of the meringue showing. Decorate with the berries or any fruit of your choice.

NOTE
You may notice some cracks in the meringue – this just makes the pavlova look more rustic and adds to the 'wow!' factor.

Rose & Pistachio Shortbread

MAKES
26

Prep 40 minutes
Cook 12 minutes

Eid is a happy time, when we prepare plates of homemade bakes for our loved ones, and the aroma of baking is ever present. These Rose & Pistachio Shortbreads are so buttery and so pretty – and there's no Eid without Eid biscuits.

Ingredients

125g unsalted butter
80g icing sugar
2 tablespoons oil
1 teaspoon rose essence
2 tablespoons ground pistachios
2 tablespoons cornflour
200g plain flour, plus extra as needed
½ teaspoon baking powder
150g white cooking chocolate
2 tablespoons chopped pistachios
2 tablespoons dried rose petals

Method

Preheat the oven to 160°C (gas mark 3). Line a baking sheet with baking paper.

Cream the butter and icing sugar together until light and fluffy using an electric hand whisk or wooden spoon. Pour in the oil and rose essence and whisk for another minute. Stir in the ground pistachios, cornflour, plain flour and baking powder and mix with your hands to form a soft, pliable dough. If the dough is too soft, add a little more flour.

Using a rolling pin, roll out the dough on a lightly floured surface to around 5mm thickness. Cut out your desired shapes with a cookie cutter and place on the baking sheet, leaving space between each one. Set the shortbreads in the fridge to chill for a short while to prevent them spreading too much in the oven.

Bake for 12 minutes, until lightly golden at the edges. Set aside to cool on a cooling rack.

Place the chocolate in a heatproof bowl over a pan of simmering water, making sure the bowl doesn't touch the water, until the chocolate is melted. Dip half of each piece of shortbread into the chocolate and sprinkle over the chopped pistachios and rose petals so they stick to the chocolate. Stored in an airtight container, these will keep for up to a week.

Chocolate Coconut Squares

MAKES
25

Prep 30 minutes
Cook 15 minutes

These chocolate coconut squares are so crumbly and delicious. Go on, try them out – they're so moreish, you won't be able to stop eating them!

Ingredients

125g unsalted butter

80g caster sugar

1 teaspoon vanilla essence

100g desiccated coconut, plus extra for decoration

130g plain flour

1 teaspoon baking powder

2 tablespoons cocoa powder

2 x 150g packs milk cooking chocolate

Method

Preheat the oven to 160°C (gas mark 3). Grease and line a 20 x 20cm square tin with baking paper.

Cream the butter and sugar together until light and fluffy using an electric hand whisk or wooden spoon. Add the vanilla essence, desiccated coconut, plain flour, baking powder and cocoa powder and mix together to form a soft dough.

Transfer the dough to your prepared tin and press it down into a compact, even layer with the back of a spoon or your fingers.

Bake for 15 minutes, then remove from the oven and leave to cool in the tin for 1 hour.

Place the chocolate in a heatproof bowl over a pan of simmering water, making sure the bowl doesn't touch the water, until the chocolate is melted. Pour the melted chocolate over the top of the cooled base, smoothing it out into an even layer. Sprinkle over some desiccated coconut to decorate.

Allow time for the chocolate to set, then cut into 25 squares. The squares will keep for up to a week in an airtight container.

Melting Moments

Prep 40 minutes
Cook 12 minutes

MAKES
26

These buttery, shortbread-style cookies are baked to golden perfection, and the texture is so delicate, they quite literally melt in your mouth. My children love making them with me and getting involved with the Eid baking – there is something wonderful about the togetherness of family, creating fun and happy memories. And they're also perfect for gifting!

Ingredients

125g unsalted butter
80g icing sugar
2 tablespoons oil
1 teaspoon vanilla essence
30g cornflour
130g plain flour
½ teaspoon baking powder

Method

Preheat the oven to 160°C (gas mark 3). Line a baking sheet with baking paper.

Cream the butter and icing sugar together until light and fluffy using an electric hand whisk or wooden spoon. Pour in the oil and vanilla essence and whisk again for 1 minute.

Add the cornflour, plain flour and baking powder and mix to form a dough soft enough to be able to pipe with a piping bag.

Transfer the dough into a piping bag fitted with a large star-tip nozzle. Pipe 4cm star shapes onto the prepared baking sheet leaving a 3cm gap in between each, as they do spread a little.

Bake for 10–12 minutes, until lightly golden. Leave to cool on a cooling rack. These biscuits will keep for up to a week in an airtight container.

 TIP To make them look pretty, once the biscuits have cooled down, melt 150g white or milk cooking chocolate, spread a little chocolate on the top of each biscuit and add the decoration of your choice.

DESSERTS
in 5

✦ • • • • ✦ • • • • ✦

During Ramadan, our iftar meal typically ends with a sweet treat. This is a tradition that goes back as far as I can remember, and still continues today. In this chapter you will find a selection of delightful desserts; from classics to innovative new creations, not only are they effortless and easy, but they also prove that you can satisfy your sweet cravings with just 5 ingredients.

Tiramisu

Prep 20 minutes
Chill 1 hour

SERVES
5

········◆·······◆·······◆·······◆·······◆·······◆·······◆········

This eggless no-bake dessert of silky mascarpone layered between coffee-soaked sponge fingers is so indulgent yet so easy. What I love about tiramisu is that it's a fuss-free dessert and adaptable to whatever ingredients you have at home. Here, I have used condensed milk, which adds sweetness as well as creaminess, and served the dessert in individual cups to add a twist to this Italian classic.

Ingredients

400g mascarpone cheese
150g condensed milk
20 sponge fingers
4g instant coffee granules mixed with 150ml hot water
coffee powder or cocoa powder, for sprinkling

Method

In a bowl, whisk together the mascarpone cheese and condensed milk until smooth, making sure you don't over mix, which can result in a runny consistency.

Break the sponge fingers in half and dip them in the coffee liquid. Place a single layer of the fingers in the base of each dessert cup or bowl and top with 3 tablespoons of the mascarpone mixture, then repeat the layers again. I used 8 sponge finger halves per dessert cup – 4 for the base and 4 for the second layer.

Set in the fridge for 1 hour. Before serving, dust the top of each cup with sieved coffee powder or cocoa powder.

 Grate some chocolate over the top for added deliciousness!

NOTE

You can adjust the sweetness of this dessert by adding more or less of the condensed milk. In addition, you can adjust the amount of coffee, depending on how strong you want the flavour.

No-Bake Rasmalai Milk Cake

Prep 20 minutes
Chill 1 hour

Rasmalai is a royal and classic Indian dessert, normally served at special occasions and get-togethers. Made with milk powder or cottage cheese, these dumplings are gently simmered in sweet, thickened milk which is delicately fragranced with cardamom and saffron. They are left to soak in the milk and are so soft and spongey, often garnished with chopped pistachios and almonds. If you're a fan of rasmalai, then you are in for a treat. This is one of my favourite milk cake flavours – perfect for when you're entertaining guests, especially when you don't have a lot of time. It is the most delightful, delicious and simple dessert.

Ingredients

12 shop-bought Madeira sponge cake slices, or any plain cake slices

300g evaporated milk

140g condensed milk

½ teaspoon cardamom seeds, crushed, plus extra for decoration

250ml double cream

6 pistachio nuts, chopped, to garnish (optional)

Method

Lay the sponge slices in the base of a 23 x 30cm glass dish and set aside.

Place a small saucepan on a low heat and pour in the evaporated milk, condensed milk and crushed cardamom seeds. Heat through gently for 2–3 minutes.

Pour the milk mixture over the sponge slices and set aside to allow them to soak up the mixture.

Using an electric hand whisk, whip the cream to soft peaks. Spread the whipped cream evenly over the soaked sponges, then sprinkle a little cardamom over the top and garnish with chopped pistachios, if desired.

Leave in the fridge for 1 hour and enjoy chilled.

 Make this dish a day ahead. The sponges will really soak up the milk, resulting in a light and soft texture and a dessert that is easy to slice.

Fruity Custard

Prep 15 minutes
Cook 15 minutes
Chill 1 hour

SERVES

4

I'm going totally old-school with this smooth, creamy, fruity custard dessert. Growing up, I remember my grandmother making this whenever we had guests. It's the easiest and tastiest dessert you'll ever find.

Ingredients

3 heaped tablespoons custard powder
3 tablespoons granulated sugar
600ml milk
1 banana, sliced
415g tin of fruit cocktail, drained

Method

Place the custard powder and sugar in a small bowl. Add 3 tablespoons of the milk and mix to a smooth paste.

Heat the remaining milk in a saucepan to nearly boiling point, then turn off the heat. Pour in the custard paste, stirring continuously. Cook on a low heat, until the custard starts to thicken. Make sure to keep stirring so the custard doesn't become lumpy, stick to the pan or burn.

Set aside to cool completely before adding the sliced banana and fruit cocktail. Chill in the fridge for an hour before serving.

 Sprinkle over chocolate curls or grated chocolate to decorate.

 You could also use fresh fruits, such as chopped strawberries, blueberries, mango and apple.

Chocolate Biscuit Cheesecake

Prep 15 minutes
Chill 1-2 hours

These decadent single-serve cheesecake cups are made from layers of chocolate biscuit crumbs, chocolate cream cheese filling and fresh strawberries. Perfect for special occasions like Eid, weddings, parties, or when you are simply looking to indulge in yourself, they are simply divine.

Ingredients

16 cookies and cream biscuits (I use Oreos)
550ml double cream
200g cream cheese
150g chocolate spread (I use Nutella)
400g fresh strawberries, plus an extra 5 to garnish

Method

In a food processor, blitz the biscuits until you have fine crumbs.

To make the cheesecake, place 250ml double cream, the cream cheese and chocolate spread in a bowl. Using an electric hand whisk, whip everything until smooth and creamy, about 2 minutes; the consistency should be fairly thick, though not stiff.

Set aside the 5 strawberries for garnish and slice the remainder into small chunks.

Leaving about 5 tablespoons for garnish, divide the biscuit crumbs between 5 dessert cups and press down using the back of a spoon. Spread the chocolate cream cheese mixture onto the biscuit bases and smooth over using the back of a spoon. Sprinkle over some strawberry pieces– it doesn't have to look too neat!

Whisk the remaining cream using an electric hand whisk until soft peaks form. You can use a spoon to spread the cream over the top of the cups, or use a piping bag with a large star nozzle to pipe pretty swirls on top. Decorate with biscuit crumbs and two strawberry halves to add a finishing touch. Transfer to the fridge for 1–2 hours or overnight and serve chilled.

Caramelised Biscuit & Banana Cheesecake

SERVES
6

Prep 35 minutes
Chill 1–2 hours

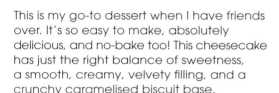

This is my go-to dessert when I have friends over. It's so easy to make, absolutely delicious, and no-bake too! This cheesecake has just the right balance of sweetness, a smooth, creamy, velvety filling, and a crunchy caramelised biscuit base.

Ingredients

14 caramelised biscuits (I use Biscoff biscuits)
250ml double cream
200g cream cheese
200g biscuit spread (I use smooth Biscoff spread)
2 bananas, sliced

TOPPING
300ml double cream
1 banana, sliced
3 tablespoons biscuit spread (I use Biscoff spread)

Method

In a food processor, blitz the caramelised biscuits until you have fine crumbs.

To make the cheesecake, place the double cream, cream cheese and biscuit spread in a bowl. Using an electric hand whisk, whip everything until smooth and creamy, about 2 minutes; the consistency should be fairly thick, though not stiff.

Divide the biscuit crumbs between 6 dessert cups or bowls and press down using the back of a spoon. Spread the cream cheese mixture over the biscuit bases and smooth using the back of a spoon, then place banana slices on top – it doesn't have to look too neat!

For the topping, whisk the cream using an electric hand whisk until soft peaks form. You can use a spoon to spread the cream over the top of the cups, or use a piping bag with a large star nozzle to pipe pretty swirls on top. Place a banana slice on top of each one to garnish. Transfer to the fridge for 1–2 hours or overnight and serve chilled.

In a heatproof bowl, melt the biscuit spread in the microwave for 20 seconds. Fill a piping bag with the melted spread and drizzle over your desserts.

 TIP You can also use Digestive biscuits for this recipe, which taste just as good.

Knafeh Nests

Prep 20 minutes
Cooks 30 minutes

MAKES
6

Knafeh is a Middle Eastern delicacy, made with fine, vermicelli-like, shredded filo dough, filled with cheese, baked until crisp and golden and drenched in sugar syrup to add sweetness. Traditionally made and served on a shallow silver plate, I first tried knafeh in Istanbul many years ago, and oh my… I really enjoyed it. This mini version is the perfect individual portion size to serve for your guests.

Ingredients

160ml water
100g granulated sugar
150g kataifi pastry (shredded filo dough)
3 heaped tablespoons ghee, melted, plus extra for greasing
130g ricotta cheese
ground pistachios, for decoration (optional)
dried rose petals, for decoration (optional)

Method

Preheat the oven to 190°C (gas mark 5).

In a medium saucepan, heat the water and sugar on a medium heat until the sugar has dissolved, then turn off the heat and let the syrup cool.

Place the kataifi pastry in a large bowl and shred the dough using your fingers. Add the melted ghee and mix with your hands so the ghee is well incorporated.

Using a pastry brush, coat the 6 muffin tray holes with ghee. Add about 2 tablespoons of kataifi pastry into each muffin hole. Press it down firmly using your fingers, bringing the knafeh dough around the sides of the holes as well.

Fill the middle of each pastry nest with a heaped tablespoon of ricotta cheese, and cover with more kataifi pastry on top, pressing down gently with your fingers.

Bake for 30–35 minutes until golden brown. Remove from the oven and immediately pour the syrup over the knafeh. These are best eaten fresh out of the oven. If you like, you can decorate with ground pistachios or dried rose petals.

 If you like chocolate, you could fill these with chocolate spread instead of ricotta, and drizzle over melted chocolate or Nutella.

 Add 1 teaspoon of rose essence or orange blossom water to the sugar syrup, to add a hint of floral aroma and taste.

Crushed Pineapple Dream

SERVES
8

Prep 30 minutes
Chill 1-2 hours

The taste of pineapple is a fusion of sweet and slightly tart flavours, and there is no better way to use it than in this fuss-free dessert. I love fruity, creamy desserts, as the mousse-like texture is so delicate, light and fluffy and bursting with freshness, while the soured cream gives it serious depth and flavour. I used tinned pineapple, but you could use fresh, if you prefer.

Ingredients

300ml double cream
300ml soured cream
160g condensed milk
500g tinned crushed pineapple, drained, plus extra to garnish
1 pack of flakey chocolate, to garnish (I use Flake)

Method

Place the double cream, soured cream and condensed milk in a large bowl and use an electric whisk to whip everything until soft peaks form.

Fold the crushed pineapple into the cream mixture until well combined.

Transfer the mixture into a dish, approximately 30 x 22cm. Spread the mixture evenly using the back of a spoon. Add a little extra tinned pineapple to garnish, then transfer to the fridge for 1–2 hours until chilled.

Crumble the chocolate over the top and serve.

NOTE
You can also use tinned pineapple chunks or slices, just keep some aside for decoration and blitz the rest in a food processor.

 TIP Add some crushed biscuits alongside the chocolate on top, if you like some crunch to it!

Creamy Mango Delight

SERVES
5

Prep 20 minutes
Chill 1 hour

When I went to India, my grandparents would pick fresh mangoes off their tree for us to enjoy. I've been fascinated with their taste, colour and aroma ever since, and have been inspired to use them in desserts whenever I can. The best mangoes to use for this dessert are Kesar or Alphonso, both of which originated in India and are juicy and delicious. Your family is in for a delightful surprise.

Ingredients

5 mini Madeira cakes, or any plain cakes

3 mangoes – 2 peeled and flesh sliced; 1 peeled and flesh cut into small chunks

200ml double cream

2 tablespoons icing sugar

5 raspberries

Method

Crumble the sponge cakes into the base of a 15 x 20cm glass dish and spread evenly over the bottom.

Add the sliced mango flesh to a blender and blend until puréed. Set aside.

Using an electric hand whisk, whip the double cream and sugar together until soft peaks form. Stir in the mango purée, leaving about 4 tablespoons aside for decoration.

Spread the mango cream mixture evenly over the crumbled cake. Add the mango chunks and raspberries on top, and drizzle over the remaining mango purée.

Leave in the fridge for 1 hour to set, and serve chilled.

 This dessert can be made in advance. Just keep it chilled in the fridge until ready to use.

 Garnish with a mint sprig to add an extra finishing touch.

Avocado Surprise

Prep 15 minutes
Chill 1 hour

SERVES
3

If you like avocados, you will love this quick and easy dessert. My mother-in-law made this often, and it's my daughter's favourite – she's nicknamed it 'the gloopy dessert'.

Ingredients

3 avocados
300ml milk
4 tablespoons granulated sugar

Method

Cut 2 avocados in half lengthways, remove the seed carefully, and use a spoon to scoop the flesh into a blender.

Add the milk and sugar and blend until smooth and creamy.

Divide between individual dessert bowls and chill for 1 hour. When ready to serve, cut the remaining avocado in half lengthways, remove the seed carefully, and chop the flesh into small cubes. Scatter over the top of the bowls to decorate.

Drinks

✦ ·◦·◦· ✦ ·◦·◦· ✦

You'll find yourself amazed by the trendy, vibrant and refreshing drinks in this chapter, from smooth and creamy milkshakes to tantalising fruity and zingy mocktails. Whether you're hosting, sharing with loved ones or just relaxing by yourself, these refreshments will elevate every occasion.

Roseberry Mocktail

Prep 10 minutes

I love the combination of rose and raspberries. It creates a beautiful blend of flavour – the delicate floral taste of the rose syrup, the sweetness of the raspberries – and vibrant colour. This beautiful and fragrant mocktail will surely stand out on your dinner table, creating a feast for the eyes.

Ingredients

1 tablespoon rose syrup

6 raspberries

1 tablespoon fresh mint leaves

½ lime, thinly sliced

sparkling water, to top up

ice cubes, to serve

rosemary sprig, to garnish

Method

Place the rose syrup, raspberries, mint leaves and lime slices in a tall glass.

Muddle the contents of the glass with the tip of a wooden spoon to crush and release the oils and juices.

Top up with sparkling water and add some ice cubes. Garnish with a sprig of rosemary to add that extra touch.

Mango & Passion Fruit Mocktail

SERVES

1

Prep 10 minutes

Lush and juicy mangoes and the tangy-sweet flavour of passion fruit add an exotic twist to this mocktail. The aroma of mint and the zesty burst of the lime really enhance the taste, which is finished off with the refreshing fizz of the sparkling water.

Ingredients

1 ripe mango, peeled and flesh cut into chunks
2 passion fruits
1 tablespoon fresh mint leaves, plus extra to garnish
½ lime, thinly sliced
sparkling water, to top up
ice cubes, to serve

Method

Place the mangoes, the pulp of 1 passion fruit and mint leaves in a tall glass. Set aside 1 lime slice to garnish, then add the remaining slices to the glass.

Muddle the contents of the glass with the tip of a wooden spoon to crush and release the oils and juices. Top up with sparkling water and ice cubes.

To garnish, cut off the bottom third of the passion fruit. Put the remaining passion fruit pulp in the drink and place the bottom third on top of your drink for decoration. Make a cut halfway through the lime slice, from the centre to the edge, and slide it onto the edge of your glass. Finish with a mint sprig for that extra touch. Enjoy!

 To add extra sweetness to your mocktail, and to pretty up your drink, run a lime wedge around the rim of the glass and dip the wet rim into some sugar before preparing the drink.

Strawberry Heaven Mocktail

Prep 10 minutes

This mocktail is inspired by a lime and mint Mojito mocktail, with a vibrant fresh and fruity twist. It's so refreshing and guaranteed to cool you down and give you summer vibes.

Ingredients

1 tablespoon strawberry syrup

3 large strawberries, hulled

1 tablespoon fresh mint leaves, plus an extra sprig to garnish

1 lime, thinly sliced

100ml lemonade

ice cubes, to serve

Method

Place the strawberry syrup, strawberries and mint leaves into a tall glass. Set aside 1 lime slice to garnish, then add the remaining slices to the glass.

Muddle the contents of the glass with the tip of a wooden spoon to crush and release the oils and juices. Top up with lemonade and add some ice cubes. Garnish with a sprig of mint and a lime slice.

Coconut Crunch Milkshake

SERVES

1

Prep 5 minutes

My children absolutely love this creamy, crunchy milkshake. With its rich, nutty flavour, it's a tasty treat for any occasion.

Ingredients

100g vanilla ice cream

100ml full-fat milk

1 coconut chocolate bar (I use Bounty 57g bar)

chocolate sauce, for drizzling

DECORATION

Whipped cream

Chocolate curls

Method

Add the ice cream, milk and chocolate bar to a blender and blend for 12 seconds.

Drizzle a little chocolate sauce inside a tall glass before pouring in the milkshake. Serve straight away, topped with whipped cream and chocolate curls.

Strawberry Milkshake

Prep 5 minutes

SERVES

1

A milkshake is a timeless classic, and sweet strawberries and creamy ice cream make the perfect duo. My dad made the best milkshake, and my brother and I would drink it in the sunshine in the garden. This drink brings back so many good childhood memories – it's a truly enjoyable treat for all the family.

Ingredients

7 large strawberries, hulled
100g vanilla ice cream, plus an extra scoop, to serve
120ml full-fat milk
strawberry sauce, for drizzling

Method

Place 6 strawberries, the ice cream and milk in a blender and blend until smooth.

Drizzle a little strawberry sauce inside a tall glass before pouring in the milkshake. Top with a scoop of ice cream and decorate with a strawberry. You can drizzle a little more strawberry sauce on top, if you like.

Mango Lassi

Prep 10 minutes

SERVES
1

Mango lassi is a family favourite, a cool, rich, creamy drink. Fresh, sweet mango is blended with yogurt and a hint of cardamom, resulting in a velvety-smooth texture. This refreshing and hydrating drink is perfect during Ramadan, helping to quench your thirst after a day of fasting.

Ingredients

1 ripe mango, peeled and flesh cut into chunks

2 tablespoons Greek yogurt

1 tablespoon granulated sugar

¼ teaspoon cardamom seeds, crushed, plus a little extra to garnish

100ml full-fat milk, plus extra if needed

salt, to taste

Method

Set aside a few mango chunks to decorate. Place the remaining mango chunks, yogurt, sugar, cardamom and milk in a blender and blend until smooth. Add a little extra milk if it's too thick for you.

Pour into a glass, decorate with mango chunks and sprinkle over a little cardamom.

Reader Recipes

I hope in this cookbook you've found lots of new favourites to share with your family and friends. But I also know there are recipes you'll have eaten as a child that you'll want to keep safe for future generations. This is why I've left some pages at the back of my book where you can write them down.

NAME

SERVES

TIME

Ingredients

Method

NAME

SERVES

TIME

Ingredients

Method

SERVES

TIME

Ingredients

Method

Ingredients

Method

Ingredients

Method

NAME

SERVES

TIME

Ingredients

Method

Ingredients

Method

SERVES

TIME

Ingredients

Method

Ingredients

Method

Ingredients

Method

Index

D

E

R

S

Acknowledgements

I am forever thankful to the Almighty, who has blessed me with the strength, encouragement, inspiration and guidance to go through life, with loving friends and family to be my amazing support network and to have a positive influence on me.

A special thanks to my super amazing husband, Adam. I am so grateful and appreciate you standing by my side over the years since day one. Whenever I've really needed someone in my corner, you have always been there. Thanks for supporting me in every aspect of my life. Always motivating me to chase my dreams and to never give up! Always keeping it honest and real with me but also having confidence in me even when I've sometimes doubted myself. Thank you for being there every step of the way. Teamwork definitely makes the dream work!

I am truly grateful to my beloved mum and gran for teaching me the basic skills of cooking. They let me explore and take over the kitchen and make a mess, just so I could learn and find out what food is all about. What family and food means. They are the reason I was able to gather so many of my favourite childhood recipes and share them in both my first book and this cookbook.

My amazing dad has taught me respect, manners and so much more that has helped me in my life. And to my one and only dear brother who always showed up whenever I needed anything. Thanks for being you!

I want to thank my dear mother-in-law for sharing her recipes, cooking styles and techniques so that I could share them with you all; and my dear father-in-law for his support and guidance, always encouraging me to never say no to opportunities that come my way.

Special thanks to my children. My super talented and creative daughter, who has helped me with recipe testing, with her artistic diagrams for the book, and offered a helping hand around the home to make my life so much easier.

My handsome and bright sons for taking an interest in what I do, for giving me quirky ideas for different recipes – and giving me honest feedback. For always keeping me smiling with their funny, quick-witted humour.

To all my family, aunts, uncles, cousins and beautiful friends, for always cheering me on and being so supportive throughout my journey.

To my incredible and super awesome management team, Reza, Omar and Saif, for always being helpful and looking after my interests, handling my day-to-day communications, campaigns and projects, and generally being there for me and making my professional life a bit easier to handle.

A big thank you to Ru, for having faith in me, for kick-starting my book journey and making it all happen! This was something I always wanted to do but didn't know how. Thank you so much for recognising my work. Thank you to the whole Ebury Team, Lara, Mia, Alice and Sam, and for all your patience, guidance and care throughout the process, to make this dream of mine come true. You are amazing!

Massive thanks to the team behind the scenes, Ellis, Sonali, Sophie, Maria, and Shasmin, for bringing my cookbooks to life and making them look so perfect, a joy to flick through, and so beautiful inside and out for readers to enjoy.

I am grateful from the bottom of my heart to all my followers and readers around the world. Thank you for supporting me in my journey right from the start, when I used to make cringy YouTube videos! You have been amazing. Thanks for keeping me going, and for all the wonderful support and praise everyone has given on my first cookbook, too. I couldn't have done it without you!

About the Author

Anisa Karolia is one of the UK's most popular Muslim food bloggers, sharing all of her favourite authentic recipes since 2015. She has a community of over 240,000 followers worldwide and was a British Muslim Award winner for Online Personality of the Year in 2023.

Through her various platforms, Anisa's mission is to share quick and easy recipes, and she especially loves to share those all-time family favourites that she enjoyed growing up with.

www.cookwithanisa.com

𝕏 @cookwithanisa
⧉ @anisagrams
▶ @cookwithanisa

Also available now!

• • ✦ • •

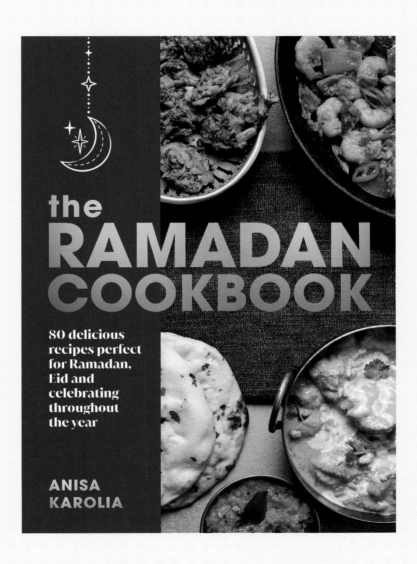

the
RAMADAN
COOKBOOK

**80 delicious
recipes perfect
for Ramadan,
Eid and
celebrating
throughout
the year**

**ANISA
KAROLIA**

1

Published in 2024 by Ebury Press an imprint of Ebury Publishing
20 Vauxhall Bridge Road
London SW1V 2SA

Ebury Press is part of the Penguin Random House group of companies
whose addresses can be found at global.penguinrandomhouse.com

First published by Ebury Press in 2024

www.penguin.co.uk

A CIP catalogue record for this book is available from the British Library

ISBN 9781529928631

Design: Studio Noel
Photography: Ellis Parrinder
Food styling: Sonali Shah
Food styling assistants: Sophie Pryn & Maria Gurevich
Prop styling: Lauren Miller

Printed and bound in Great Britain by Bell & Bain Ltd

The authorised representative in the EEA is Penguin Random House
Ireland, Morrison Chambers, 32 Nassau Street, Dublin D02 YH68

Penguin Random House is committed to a
sustainable future for our business, our readers
and our planet. This book is made from Forest
Stewardship Council® certified paper.